BREAKING THE SLUMP

HOW GREAT PLAYERS SURVIVED THEIR DARKEST MOMENTS IN GOLF—AND WHAT YOU CAN LEARN FROM THEM

JIMMY ROBERTS

HARPER

NEW YORK · LONDON · TORONTO · SYDNEY

HARPER

A hardcover edition of this book was published in 2009 by Collins, an imprint of HarperCollins Publishers.

HarperCollins books may be purchased for educational, business, or sales promotional use. For information please write: Special Markets Department, HarperCollins Publishers, 10 East 53rd Street, New York, NY 10022.

FIRST HARPER PAPERBACK PUBLISHED 2011.

Library of Congress Cataloging-in-Publication Data is available upon request.

ISBN 978-0-06-168600-9

11 12 13 14 15 OV/RRD 10 9 8 7 6 5 4 3 2 1

To Ralph and Betty for showing me the way.

To Jackson, Aidan, and Daniel for filling each step with such joy.

And most of all to Sandy for everything . . . and so much more.

CONTENTS

INTRODUCTION
Slump

"I'm one bad swing away from antiquing!"

I don't know that the details really matter all that much. I imagine it's happened to anybody who's ever been foolish enough to allow this game to matter to the extent we all do.

I am in a slump. I'd have to say it's considerable, although who has ever been in a slump they *didn't* think was considerable? This one is especially vexing because it's the "throw your clubs in the lake, never gonna play again" variety. But then again, if you play this game, I imagine you fall into one of two categories when it comes to this type of slump: either you've had one (at least one), or you're *going* to have one (at least one).

Slumps are terrible things. Just when golf has allowed you to achieve a relative level of competency, just when you've actually started to feel good about your game, they arrive out of nowhere like Marley's ghost to rattle their chains and terrify. A slump will cause the perfectly sane to talk out loud to no one in particular and without an ounce of shame. A slump can infect every aspect of your otherwise healthy life and turn even the most optimistic among us into Chicken Little.

Just as you don't talk to a major leaguer about a no-hitter while he's pitching one, you don't imply that a golfer might be suffering a slump unless it's actually sighted, confirmed, and, most importantly, *admitted* (as if the word itself might have some type of self-actualizing mystical power). PGA Tour players can be very touchy on this subject. Tiger Woods spent a good three months in the winter and spring of 2001 glowering at anybody who had the audacity to wonder if he might be slumping. He'd gone winless for one of the longest stretches of his young career, but then rattled off three straight triumphs at Bay Hill, the Players, and the Masters. That year I got the "wrong place, wrong time" award when Woods, after winning the Players Championship, turned contemptuously to me in the post-tournament interview and said, "Nice slump, huh Jimmy?" then sullenly stormed off.

(For the record, many people that fall had suggested Woods was enduring a slump, but I was *not* one of them. The closest I got was joking a few weeks earlier during the Tour's stop at Doral that Woods was in a slump about the same way the Beatles were slumping in any given week in 1964 when they *didn't* have a number one record.)

On and off, I've been playing golf since I was seven.

When I was fourteen, I won our club junior nine-hole tournament. When I was forty-two, I had my first (and so far only) hole-in-one. Those two facts might lead you to believe I can play, that perhaps I'm one of those awful people who plops down next to you in the grill room with a dour face, complaining about the "horrible" 79 he's just chopped his way through.

Actually, where I come from, there's no such thing as a horrible 79. I am mediocre at best. My greatest accomplishment in the game was vowing to get my USGA Handicap Index down to single digits before my fiftieth birthday—and actually doing so.

I grew up a child of relative privilege in Westchester County, New York, about forty-five minutes north of New York City. We belonged to a country club, and every weekend my father played. He had the most amazing swing: the takeaway was the slowest, most deliberate move you could ever imagine. But once he got to the top, there was a frightening explosive contraction that made you think perhaps someone had fired a gun at the swing's apogee—only my father had heard it—and it had scared the shit out of him. Think a slower version of Ernie Els on the backswing and a faster version of Hubert Green going the other way. Dad was frustrated by the game, but dedicated. One year he won the "C" flight of the club championship. After Dad's teaching me didn't quite work out (disaster), I ended up on the lesson tee with the head pro. Jack Kiley had slicked-back hair and wore Sansabelt pants. I imagine he had just the look that made all the Laura Petrie–type moms swoon just a little bit. I was a fairly athletic kid, and he helped me to develop a reasonable swing. But it was one that contained a near-fatal flaw: way too much lateral movement. In the parlance of the industry, there was too much sliding, and not enough rotation. The result was a slice I would fight for the next thirty-five years.

As a teenager I settled into a niche of comfortable incompetence. I shot mostly around 100, never serious enough about the game to pursue a remedy for a swing that grew more and more broken. I loved the game, loved being on the course with my friends, but life was too busy to devote the requisite time to correct the problem. Something as simple as changing my grip just felt like more trouble than it was worth. My diseased swing felt completely natural, and while changing it might eventually yield results, it wouldn't be fun. It would be work. So I dawdled along in the neighborhood of three digits until a reason arose for me to change things.

In the spring of 2000, I joined NBC Sports. I would cover Wimbledon and the Olympics, major league baseball, and a few other things, but mostly I would cover golf.

That meant joining a broadcast team that not only loved the game but also played it at every possible opportunity. For the twelve previous years at ESPN and ABC,

I might have played a total of fifteen rounds of golf while on the road covering big events. NBC was a totally different animal. The first event I worked for my new employer was the 2000 U.S. Open at Pebble Beach. In my first four days on the job, I played four rounds of golf: Spanish Bay, Del Monte, Cypress Point, and Pebble Beach. The round at Pebble on my very first day of work proved to be the slap in the face that changed my attitude about the game.

That Saturday morning, we recorded our U.S. Open preview show. I joined host Dan Hicks and expert commentators Roger Maltbie, Gary Koch, and Mark Rolfing as we shot the on-camera portions of the show just off of Pebble's ninth green. When we finished, producer Tom Roy clapped his hands and shouted, "All right, good job everybody. We've got two foursomes. We better hustle over to the first tee."

Now there are a few things to understand about what was about to happen. I was going to play golf with my new colleagues. Not only was this one of the hardest golf courses I had ever seen, but the custom among this group was to play it all the way back: ALL THE WAY. Those in the group who weren't former touring pros like Maltbie and Koch were just *really* good, like Tom Randolph, our co-producer, who was an all-America, honorable mention at UCLA, and captain of a golf team that would include future PGA Tour winners Corey Pavin, Steve Pate, and Tom Pernice. Roy, my boss, was the son of a golf pro, who himself once harbored an ambition to try and play the Tour. So here I was, nervous and overmatched. I'd like to say the next four and a half hours went well. They didn't. "Catastrophe" would have been a charitable characterization. Talk about a good walk spoiled: the low point came on the twelfth hole. As I stood on the tee box of the par three, out popped Maltbie, who had decided not to play. Just as I sent a hozel-rocket screaming to the right at shoetop level, I looked up to see him laughing hysterically. And there in his hand was a small camera. I wish it was only humiliating, but it seemed so much worse. Hole by hole, I felt my credibility with my new colleagues slowly evaporating. As I walked alone to find my ball I could only imagine what they were thinking: "Why would we ever hire this clown? He could be the worst golfer I've ever seen."

Beautiful afternoon, incredible place, and it was the worst single day I've ever had on a golf course. I vowed that afternoon I would never be humiliated like that again. And so like some golfing Rocky Balboa, I started looking for museum steps to run and sides of beef to hit. I took lessons with Harvey Lannak, an incredible instructor at Westchester Country Club, and I watched my friend Gary Koch closely each time we went to play, and then leaned heavily on his expertise. I spent hours on the range at PGA Tour events watching the best swings on Planet Earth and then ran back and tried to duplicate what I had observed. Butch Harmon looked at my swing. So did David Ledbetter and Peter Kostis. But mostly I just beat balls. My climb out of the morass was long and ugly.

A trip to play a handful of the great courses on the east end of New York's Long Island comes to mind. The Hamptons is a bucolic playground for the well-to-do, known for many genteel country pursuits aside from exclusive golf courses like Shinnecock, National Golf Links, and the Maidstone Club. So when another feeble and cringe-worthy effort dribbled off the heel of my driver, I let out a primal and frustrated scream that still haunts me among my golf buddies today:

"I'm one bad swing away from antiquing!" I exploded. But slowly—very slowly—I got better, and the watershed moments took on an altogether different character.

One year, I played in the Pro-Am at the Arnold Palmer Invitational at Bay Hill. I went to the range early and tried to find the most distant corner in which to warm up. Just as I was almost through, I heard a mocking nasal twang: "Oh, this ought to be good. Let's see what you got."

It was Fred Couples, and he had rounded up a handful of other players. I would have much rather simply left them with the mistaken notion I was a good player than hit even one shot and demonstrate I was not, but they were having none of it. Finally, I stuck a tee in the ground and, with sweat pouring down my forehead, hit a very respectable drive with a nice soft fade. I picked up the tee, put my driver back in my bag, and confidently strutted past the now-silent golfers.

"So, Fred," I said. "I guess the next time you shoot 79, I can insist you stop by to talk with me, right?"

I didn't suck anymore.

And that's the world I lived in for a few years. Golf was exciting. I didn't count my score on each hole in relation to "fives" anymore. The game was now about the pursuit of par. Now that I could hit the ball, I worked on the subtleties of the game: bunker play, trajectory, flop shots. One day I looked up on the range and realized my ball flight was no longer left to right. My god, I was drawing the ball!

I wasn't going on tour, but I was solidly in the mid-eighties. My handicap sank to 9.8. Life was good. And then something happened.

That nice draw suddenly turned into a hook, and then a vicious hook. My driver, which had always been the most dependable club in my bag, betrayed me and started producing the most ungodly thing: a short, high pull—with a tail! I ran to Harvey for help, and he fixed things temporarily, but a day later, I was a mess again. Marley's ghost had arrived.

I haven't yet figured this thing out, but I know I will. I hope I will. Intellectually, I'm confident I can get through it, but despite what I've found myself saying on television dozens of times, there is absolutely no cerebral component to success in this game.

It's all voodoo.

And just as we all stand on the range looking into each other's bags to see what type of equipment the next guy is using, I want to know what kind of voodoo others have summoned in their darkest hours. So I packed my bag and headed out to collect slump stories. If for some reason I can't beat this thing by myself, maybe I can learn from somebody else. I went knocking on the doors of not only golf's legends but also those enormously successful and celebrated in other endeavors who also just happen to be obsessed with the game as well.

What was your worst slump? Did you ever lose hope? How did you pull yourself out of it? How long did it take? I had a million questions. Perhaps the answers would shine a light for me on the path out of the darkness. Maybe they will for you too.

Chapter 1

PAUL AZINGER

*"Confidence is something that when you have it,
you never think you're going to lose it, and when you lose it,
you never think you're going to get it back."*

It is a sunny late September morning in Bradenton, Florida, and I am standing in line at Starbucks with Captain America. I go for a decaf, but Paul Azinger prefers something stronger. As if he needs it. He's buzzing anyway.

"Way to go," an older woman yells at Azinger a few minutes later from the window of a weathered SUV. "Congratulations!"

Much to Azinger's delight and surprise, the scene is repeated a handful more times as we sit sipping our coffee at an outdoor table. "There's a lot going on that's not good," he says. "I think it's kind of a scary time, and this was uplifting for a lot of people."

Eight days earlier, using a blueprint for team building that might wow the people at Harvard Business School, Azinger engineered a win for the United States at the

Ryder Cup in Louisville, Kentucky. It had been nearly a decade since the last United States win, and America's fortunes in the competition had become something of a hyper-scrutinized obsession in the insular world of golf. So instead of sipping coffee with me on a lazy Monday morning on the Gulf Coast of Florida, Azinger could be in Los Angeles doing the *Tonight Show* with Jay Leno, or taping a guest spot with Ellen DeGeneres or Jimmy Kimmel, but he has turned it all down to come back home and just let it sink in.

"I feel like I spent the last two years slowly pulling back the string of a bow and I finally let it go."

With the Cup in tow, he will venture across town later in the week to throw out the first pitch in Game Two of the first ever major league baseball post-season series for his hometown Tampa Bay Rays. As we sit talking, his phone rattles incessantly. Hundreds of text messages, voice-mails, and e-mails have yet to be returned, including one from the president of the United States. "I don't want to call him back yet. He's so busy up there. I don't want him to feel obligated to take my call. He's got more important things to do."

The night before, we walked out his back door and onto the dock, which leads 382 feet out into Tampa Bay. The sky was clear and the night was silent, except for small waves lapping hypnotically against the pylons. Azinger looked west towards the Gulf of Mexico and sighed. "People always ask me why in the world I would want to live in Bradenton. There's nothing here. 'You're right,' I tell them. 'You don't want to come here.'"

He laughs, and we head back to the house. Life is impossibly good. Three months ago, he walked his oldest daughter down the aisle, and just seven days earlier, he cunningly led the U.S. team to a Ryder Cup win over a side captained by his long-time adversary and irritant, Nick Faldo, the man with whom he'd often sarcastically dueled as television commentators for ABC Sports. Many in American golf would have you believe that the Louisville matches were a matter of life and death. Azinger is a vicious competitor, and he desperately wanted to win the Ryder Cup, but it was hardly a life-and-death affair. Who in golf could possibly know that any better?

There was a time not too long before when Azinger's celebrity wasn't about helping *others* do their best, or commenting about it on TV, but rather doing it himself.

In 1987, he was the PGA of America's Player of the Year. It was the start of a muscular seven-year stretch during which he collected eleven wins on Tour and finished every year except one in the top ten on the money list. The year he didn't, he finished eleventh. "If I wasn't the best player in the world, I was certainly the hottest," he says.

He might have also been the biggest surprise.

There are successful pros like Nicklaus or Mickelson or Woods who exploded through amateur and junior golf and collected every credential there was. There are players like Steve Stricker and Davis Love who had modest but successful amateur careers before they made a name in professional golf. And then there are the real rarities—players like Azinger.

"I couldn't break 80 two days in a row my senior year in high school," Azinger remembers. "I suppose I probably could, but if I did, I'd run home and tell someone."

The son of an Air Force navigator who flew C-141s in Korea and Vietnam, Azinger learned to play golf mostly on military bases. His earliest memory of the game is riding atop the pull cart his dad, Ralph, dragged around the course at Homestead Air Force Base in south Florida when Paul was three years old.

"My dad was a single-digit handicap," he says, "but my mom was better than him. She got down to like a four or five handicap."

Aside from winning several state and regional tournaments, Jean Azinger's claim to fame was playing—and with great distinction—in an exhibition with the hall-of-famer Patty Berg in 1959. Jean chipped in three times during the round, a round she played while seven months pregnant—with Paul.

Initially, though, her son's in utero training didn't seem to make much of an imprint. Paul Azinger was mostly an indifferent high school golfer.

"None of my friends played golf," he says. "I just wasn't into it."

Upon graduating from Sarasota High School in the spring of 1978, he didn't get a single scholarship offer and ended up at Brevard Community College. "I knew I wasn't any good at golf," he says. "Sometimes you think you're good and you're not. I *knew* I wasn't that good."

But things started to change in the summer of 1979, when Azinger went away from home for the first time ever and took a job as a counselor at Arnold Palmer's Golf Academy at Bay Hill in Orlando. "Actually we were more like babysitters," he says. "We'd pick these campers up, and they'd stay two weeks, and then we'd take 'em back to the airport and pick up a whole new batch. I was kind of a gofer for the [teaching] pros. We took care of the kids after the day was over. Volleyball, swimming, that type of thing."

The job paid $80 a week plus a room, but the side benefit was that whenever he could steal the time, Azinger could use the facilities. That summer, he says he "lived and breathed the game."

"Bay Hill's such a hard golf course. All of a sudden, I went back to college and I'm playing these courses, and I murdered 'em."

But also, for the first time in his life, Azinger got serious instruction. Jim Suttie, his coach at Brevard, was on the Palmer Academy staff. And in addition to working tirelessly with Azinger, Suttie introduced him to a Titusville pro named John Redmond, who would be instrumental in his development.

Azinger had arrived at Bay Hill as what he called "the third man on Brevard's C team," but soon after that summer, he was the school's number one player. "It was one of those things where my game changed so much for the better, so fast," he says, "that I didn't realize what was happening."

After one more year at Brevard, he moved on to Florida State, where he started to have his first big-time competitive success, winning the Metro Conference tournament and the Gator Invitational. But Tallahassee was just a pit stop, too. "I wasn't going to get any better there," he says, "and academically I was totally uninterested."

So in the fall of 1981, after one year at Florida State, Azinger tried his hand at professional golf. Less than two years after having broken 70 for the first time, he qualified for the PGA Tour at Waterwood National in Texas. His father convinced nine friends to kick in $3,000 each, and Azinger was staked to a start. He didn't exactly explode out of the gate with confidence.

"I didn't see myself being able to compete with those guys," he says of the players on Tour. "I didn't think I was capable—mentally or anything. I thought I was going to be too nervous a figure. No self-confidence. Self-conscious about my swing. Self-conscious about my grip."

Azinger's grip. It was the neon sign that immediately attracted the attention of most knowledgeable people when they first saw him play. His left hand was rotated dramatically over the top of the club in an exceptionally strong position. No one else at this level held the club in a remotely similar fashion. Azinger's grip was like Bob Dylan's voice—unusual, even eccentric—but it had served him well.

"I had a couple of players tell me 'you'll never be any good with that grip. You've got to change it.' They were wrong, but I didn't know they were wrong."

That first year on Tour, he earned a total of $10,000 in twenty-one events. He kept his head above water, but just barely. "My first four years as a pro," he says, "I had to file taxes, but I never had to pay anything. I just kept losing money."

Then came an odd interlude that would change his career. Azinger struck up a friendship with a man named Mac McKee, who had known Azinger's wife since she was a little girl. "He told me up front," Azinger remembers, "'I don't know one thing about golf, but I know I can make you a better golfer.'"

Azinger had reason to be doubtful. McKee was a retired boxing trainer from Blackshear, Georgia, who over the years had also earned a living as a carnival fighter. For a fee you could get in the ring with him and see how tough you were. He would take on all comers. Despite being in his mid-sixties, McKee was a physical specimen who paid great attention to working out, but his hobby was studying the mind and its part in performance.

"He used to study East German philosophy," says Azinger. "He read books about concentration and hypnosis, and progressive relaxation, and that type of thing. And he asked me if I would ever consider going deeper mentally into the game and taking a different approach."

At McKee's suggestion, Azinger began to engage in heavy visualization. After playing a practice round, he would sit up in bed at night and imagine, in sequence, every single shot he would need to play, always hitting the center of the green. And he did breathing exercises to get control of his heart rate.

"Breathe in for four counts, and then exhale in a four count, too," he says. "So that happened my third year on Tour. I started to take on a different outlook. Kind of like Tiger did when he was in third grade."

His career soon took off. For the first time in four years as a professional, he earned enough money to retain his PGA Tour playing privileges, and soon he found himself on a run that culminated with a playoff victory over Greg Norman at the 1993 PGA Championship. Once, standing on the putting green at Westchester Country Club during that period, he looked up and laughed after pouring in several consecutive ten-footers and said to me, "I'm so good. I don't know how I *ever* miss one of these things!"

Azinger was a blend of color, candor, confidence, and talent. He was at the top of his game when, like an earthquake, the ground ruptured beneath his feet and swallowed him whole.

"It was over in an instant," he says. "Just like that. I

went from the most confident player, the hottest player, to just trying to stay alive."

Plagued by almost constant shoulder pain, which had started in 1987 and had him living on anti-inflammatory medication, Azinger finally submitted to a biopsy in the fall of 1993. The test revealed cancer: non-Hodgkin's lymphoma.

"They told me it was pretty much a 90 percent chance of a complete cure," he says, "and I felt that you've got a 10 percent chance of getting a flat tire on the way home, and I figured that you *never* get a flat, so I'm probably going to be fine."

More than 1.2 million Americans are diagnosed every year with some form of cancer. The fortunate ones who do find themselves with some type of viable and effective treatment will tell you, though, that as grateful as they are, the treatment is often worse than anything they could have imagined. Azinger fell squarely in that category. But the day of his first treatment, in early December 1993, he had no idea what all the foreboding was about.

"This is a cakewalk," he told his friend Payne Stewart, who'd called that day. "Chemo was easy. It was a snap." The recollection is from Azinger's 1995 autobiography, *Zinger*. Around midnight that night, he woke up and got sick for the first time. Every fifteen minutes for the next nine hours, his body convulsed.

Azinger had six months of chemotherapy in a hospital twenty-five hundred miles from his home. "I always flew to L.A. to do them because I didn't want my kids to see me sick," he says. The routine was always the same.

"I'd fly out there to do the chemo, stay sick for two or three days, and then fly home. It was a good solid ten days before I could even hear good again."

By the end of May 1994 he was done with the chemo and radiation. A little more than two months later he made the first of four "ceremonial" appearances in PGA Tour events. He was weak, but he was hopeful and alive. A year before, he had been perhaps the best player in the world. Now, he had to start from scratch—so much was different.

For one thing, Azinger just wasn't the same person he had been before he got sick.

"I didn't have the same mental edge," he says. Before, his wife, Toni, had always thought he looked as if he was in a trance out on the golf course. He seemed that consumed. But now things felt different. "I didn't have that same 'step on your head and rip your heart out' edge. I lost that."

And it wasn't only a change in the mental aspect of the game.

"I remember at Hilton Head," he says, "I played eighteen holes, slept for three hours after I was done, got up and ate dinner, and then slept until nine o'clock the next morning. My body just needed rest."

Azinger says it took him a year and half to feel like he was getting back to normal, but on top of it all was an external factor. After winning the PGA Championship, but before he discovered he was sick, Azinger signed a lucrative contract with Callaway Golf.

"I ended up switching to this club that wasn't targeted to Tour players but was being forced on us," he says. "I love the company; I'm not trying to trash them. But when I changed equipment, it had a huge effect on my game. My swing changed. My swing was just never the same."

Candid as ever, though, Azinger says there should be no confusion about why he made the move: "I did it for the money."

By some estimates, the compensation package amounted to nearly a million dollars a year and in the neighborhood of seven million dollars in stock.

He knocked around the PGA Tour for the next half dozen years, more a journeyman than the elite stud he used to be, but he made steady progress and was getting closer. And then on October 25, 1999, the world collapsed around him again.

His good friend Payne Stewart, and his managers and friends Van Arden and Robert Fraley (if anything had ever happened to Azinger and his wife, they had made arrangements for their children to be left with the Fraleys) were killed when the small private plane in which they were flying crashed on the way from Orlando to Dallas.

"I'll never forget that day," says Azinger. He had been at Disney World with his family and had turned off his cell phone. Driving back across the state late in the afternoon, he turned it on, and the device started vibrating like mad.

"Voice-mail after voice-mail after voice-mail," he remembers.

A moment later the phone rang. It was his brother, who told him that Stewart's plane had crashed, but he didn't know more. Azinger pulled over to the side of the road and called his parents. Because they hadn't been able to reach him all day, they thought perhaps he might have been on the plane.

"My mom was bawling her head off," he says now as we sit outside the Starbucks nine years later. "When my Dad said that they're all dead, I literally fell to the ground right there at the rest stop, on my knees with my wife. I was dizzy from the emotion of it."

It was a consuming tragedy for the sport and beyond, and Azinger was at the middle of the aftermath. He delivered a moving eulogy four days later, and then golf just seemed like the furthest thing from anybody's mind.

A week and half after the millennium turned—after more than two months of grieving and questioning—Azinger went to Hawaii for the start of the PGA Tour season to try and get on with his life. Golf-wise, he'd had a decent season the year before, but it was six years since he'd returned to the Tour after his illness, and he still hadn't won. What was worse, people were *still* asking him if he felt he was all the way back. "It was terrible," he says.

In the off season, he'd switched back to the type of irons with which he'd had so much success before his illness, and in the season's very first full-field event, he opened by shooting rounds of 63 and 65. It was his lowest two consecutive rounds in more than eleven years. "Somehow things just got reprioritized," he says. "I don't know how else to describe it. Mentally I was in a better place."

Once again he was full of confidence. He won the tournament by seven strokes, the questions about his fitness stopped, and Azinger learned a lesson: "Confidence is something that when you have it, you never think you're going to lose it, and when you lose it, you never think you're going to get it back. The best thing you can do in your 'self-talk' is to remind yourself what you've done in the past. You've done this before."

It was an extraordinary story, but Azinger felt that all those who wanted to make it exclusively about his long climb back from cancer missed the point. "Hawaii was great for a lot of people—a lot of people that were close to Payne and Van and Robert. It meant a lot to all of them. It was a hard time for all of us. It was a part of the healing process. It was a feel-good time when there wasn't a lot of feel-good stuff. It went beyond me."

We are back at Azinger's house now, talking in a secret room hidden behind a wall where he keeps his golf trophies and memorabilia. It's not part of the normal house tour. Entry is by invitation only. You'd never find it in a million years.

"Bubba Watson came to visit one time when I wasn't here," he says of the PGA Tour player, "and he wanted to know where all my trophies were. He couldn't figure it out."

There is a flat screen TV and comfortable overstuffed chairs. Azinger says he comes in here often and thinks.

"I'm a little more complex than people give me credit for," he says. "I think that sometimes people think I'm just a southern dumbass in some respects."

The week before at the Ryder Cup he had proved that to be a foolish assumption. He cleverly grouped his twelve players into three teams, which practiced together every day based on style of play and compatibility, and then turned them loose. He seems to give no less thought to a visitor's questions about slumps. "A lot of times people buy equipment that puts them in a slump," he says. "If you've played well and your handicap's going up, you probably made a bad change. You have to recognize it. Just because you paid more money for a set of clubs doesn't mean they're better for you."

He also thinks that people don't think enough about visualization or shot trajectory. "If you become a trajectory-conscious player, you're less likely to hit it off line."

Spend some time with Captain America, and it's clear his mind is always working. Maybe it's the caffeine, but details aren't often overlooked. So it seems odd, when you walk out the back door toward the water, that the first few steps of the path are navigated over wide and smooth stones, but soon you encounter a gap, where there is only crushed coral beneath your feet. In the house where even a secret room was designed into the original plan, I should have known that even a "mistake" has its purpose. "I left that stone out," says Azinger, "so I'll remember Payne every time I come out here."

For Paul Azinger, the path back might seem complete, but he'll never forget that something is missing.

Chapter 2

JACK NICKLAUS

"I always felt like slumps were usually self-induced.
The first thing you've got to do when you have a problem in
golf is get away from it."

For thirty-nine years, my NBC colleague Bob Murphy has hosted a charity tournament at Del Ray Dunes Golf Club in Boynton Beach, Florida. It is one of the longest running one-day pro-ams in the country and a popular affair. Murphy, a five-time winner on Tour, is annually able to convince a good number of his fellow pros to come and play for the benefit of the Bethesda Memorial Hospital. Once again this year, cars are parked all up and down Golf Road surrounding the main entrance, where there is a slight holdup.

"May I see your ticket, please?" the security guard, a woman who looks to be in her mid-sixties asks the man driving the gold Lexus.

"Ma'am," he says politely, "I'm a player." Then he pauses, laughs, and adds, "Well, at least I used to be."

Reluctantly, she passes him through, but the scene

repeats itself at the next checkpoint, because the sixty-eight-year-old gentleman with the bad back doesn't have any credentials—at least none he can wear. It is February 11, and he is eager to hit a few practice balls before his fast-approaching tee time.

"You know," Jack Nicklaus told me in the car thirty minutes earlier on the drive down from his North Palm Beach home, "when I get out to the range, it will be the first golf ball I've hit this year."

It's actually been more than two months since he's last played.

I'm shocked. It's hard to imagine this man, who attributes a good deal of what he accomplished in the game to having "outworked" everybody else, just turning his back on his clubs. I wondered if McCartney ever let his guitar gather dust or if Picasso thought there were better ways to spend time than painting or sculpting. But then I remember what Nicklaus told me as we pulled out of his driveway that morning, about the time the best player in the world had totally lost his way.

It was 1979, and for the first time in his professional career, Nicklaus had gone a season without winning a tournament. Every previous year since turning professional in 1962, he'd actually won at least twice, but now he'd hit a serious slump. For the first time since he was eligible, he failed to make the Ryder Cup team.

"I mean, you wouldn't believe how pathetic I was," Nicklaus says.

So at the end of August that year, he laid down his clubs and, with only three exceptions, didn't touch them for four months.

"And I don't know why I picked them up those three times," he says, "I guess I had to do something. I really tried to stay totally away from it. And I went back in the first part of January [1980] and I said [to his long-time teacher]: 'OK, Jack Grout, my name is Jack Nicklaus, and I'd like to learn how to play golf.'"

"You started from scratch?" I asked with incredulity.

"I started from scratch."

Jack Nicklaus is the son of a pharmacist from Columbus, Ohio, who first broke 70 at age thirteen. The highlights of his career not only are known by most golf fans but are benchmarks for every player who followed: two US Amateur titles, seventy-three PGA Tour wins, eighteen professional majors. "He plays a game with which I'm not familiar," the great Bobby Jones once famously said upon seeing a young Nicklaus play at the Masters. It's by now a well-known story that Tiger Woods, as a child, posted Nicklaus's accomplishments above his bed as the only "to-do" list in the game that in the end would really matter. Nicklaus almost won the U.S. Open as an amateur. Two years later, when he did turn professional, his first win came at the National Championship—and in dramatic fashion. He beat Arnold Palmer, the game's most popular player, in a playoff at what basically amounted to Palmer's home course: Oakmont, outside Pittsburgh. Immediately, by his actions, Nicklaus announced himself a special player.

The wins would come in bunches, the majors as if he had scheduled their acquisition.

Although legend might have it that Nicklaus was immune to the ups and downs that affected mortals, he did encounter some early struggles. For one in particular he found an unusual remedy. In the summer of 1964, the man who would become known as the Golden Bear, because of his husky physique and bearlike power, wasn't hitting the ball the way he wanted. But then the night before the first round of the Cleveland Open, he had a dream in which he was striking it perfectly. When he woke the next morning he realized that in the dream his grip was different.

"So when I came to the course yesterday morning," he told a reporter for the Cleveland *Plain Dealer* after the second round, "I tried it the way I did it in my dream and it worked."

Yes, it did. Nicklaus opened with rounds of 68 and 65, and eventually that week he finished tied for third. By the end of the year, he had not only won his first scoring title but led the money list as well—the first of eight times he would do so.

By the late 1960s, he was battling a far more insidious problem than a cockeyed grip. After winning the 1967 U.S. Open at Baltusrol in New Jersey (breaking Ben Hogan's seventy-two-hole scoring record for the championship in the process), he went a stretch of twelve consecutive majors without winning.

"I think it was just laziness," he says, "not working very hard at it. I was complacent."

Nicklaus won his share of tournaments during that period. In fact, what he did on the PGA Tour between July 1967 and June 1970 would have been a good career for many. His win total of nine during that three-year stretch alone would have—at the time—been good enough for fifty-second place on the all-time list for victories. But then on February 19, 1970, Jack Nicklaus's life was jolted out of cruise control. His father, Charlie Nicklaus, died of cancer of the pancreas and liver. He was just fifty-six years old.

"His dad was everything," says Barbara Nicklaus. We are sitting in the kitchen of the North Palm Beach home where she and Jack have lived for close to forty years. Cali, the family's fourth golden retriever, who can answer by barking how many times Jack has won the Masters, sits curled at Barbara's feet.

"He was his best friend, he was his mentor, he was his advisor, he was all of that, and I don't think it dawned on him until then how much his dad meant to him."

Charlie Nicklaus was a gregarious man of many talents. He won the Columbus city tennis championship and played semipro football in the forerunner of the NFL. He not only introduced his son to the game of golf but also infected him with the very same incurable illness from which he himself suffered: a love of any and all sports. The younger Nicklaus was a standout in track and actually went to Ohio State on a basketball scholarship because at the time there were no scholarships for golf. Whatever the sport, Jack was willing to try it, and Charlie was willing to talk about it to just about anyone.

"Woody Hayes is actually the one that got Jack away from football. Jack loved football," says Barbara. "Woody would come into Jack's dad's drugstore, and he said, 'Let me tell you something, with that talent [for golf], you keep him as far away from football as possible.'"

So when Charlie Nicklaus passed away, his son was devastated, but he was also shaken from his professional torpor.

"I felt like he was going to be around for a long time," says Nicklaus. "My dad had really lived his life through me and my successes. I was his enjoyment and his thrill. I just felt like I didn't treat him fairly when he was alive. I was lazy. I said, 'Well, my dad would have wanted me to work a little harder, wanted me to be a little bit more of the moment, and you know, I'm not going to have this talent forever.'"

So the Bear's work ethic came out of hibernation, but at St. Andrews in July 1970, his drought of majors was nearly extended before Doug Sanders missed a three-foot putt to win on the seventy-second hole. Nicklaus won the next day in a playoff. At thirty years of age, he had won his eighth professional major championship, vaulting him past a quintet of Hall of Famers: Gene Sarazen, Sam Snead, Arnold Palmer, Harry Vardon, and Bobby Jones. He was now just one major title behind Ben Hogan and only three behind the all-time leader, Walter Hagen.

"Do you think you wanted that tournament more than any other?" I ask him.

"Yes, I think I did."

Of all his legendary golfing attributes—length, clutch putting, course management—it is often noted that Nicklaus's supreme confidence might have been the most important.

J. C. Snead once said, "He knew he was going to beat you. You knew he was going to beat you, and he knew that you knew that he was going to beat you."

"I may have been confident on the outside," says Nicklaus, "but I was never as confident as people thought I was on the inside. I didn't want to be too cocksure of what I was doing. I always felt like I could be better. I don't think I ever reached 75 percent of my potential."

Maybe that's because Nicklaus, like most of us, fell into avoidable potholes. "I always felt like slumps were usually self-induced," he says. "They came about from playing too much, not working hard enough. Not thinking about what you're doing."

But whatever struggles Nicklaus had in the first seventeen years of his professional career, they were in no way similar to what befell him in 1979. He dropped all the way to seventy-first on the money list—his first time ever outside the top ten, and his lowest ranking ever.

"I was just terrible," he said.

There was no panic, but like all issues with Nicklaus and golf, there was a theory: sometimes you just have to step away. "You can't push yourself at the level that you'll get in trouble," he believes.

So after his four-month hiatus, Nicklaus and Grout went back to the lab to embark on the most radical swing reconstruction of the Bear's career. The swing plane became flatter; the grip became stronger. Here was the most accomplished golfer of all time, a man who'd won fifteen professional majors, basically throwing everything out the window.

"Going through it, you're thinking: 'What is he doing?'" says his wife. "But he doesn't attack anything less than 110 percent, so you just knew this [slump] wasn't going to get him."

But the full-swing reconstruction was only the start,

because there was another crucial facet of Nicklaus's game that desperately needed attention.

"I mean, I couldn't chip over a bunker to save my life," he says, "or chip anyplace."

So Nicklaus called for help from his old friend Phil Rodgers, former NCAA champion, five-time winner on Tour, and, most importantly, wizard of the short game.

"Basically everything I know, I learned from Paul Runyon," says Rodgers, referring to the World Golf Hall of Fame member and former PGA champion known as "Little Poison," in part because he was deadly from close range.

The plan was for Rodgers to come and spend a couple of days with Nicklaus in Palm Beach.

"I ended up staying for more than two weeks," he says. "He [Jack] won with his power and his long game. Nobody in his time had that type of power. He could hit it over the Empire State Building. And he was a wonderful putter, maybe the best ever, especially on putts he needed to make, but he never had to rely on his short game. If you went back and watched him, you would see he would putt from [just] off the green. Chipping was always a problem."

So Rodgers taught Nicklaus some of the Runyon fundamentals: a different grip which resembled one normally used for putting and a swing to use while chipping which routed the club in something of a muted figure eight. But mostly, Rodgers says he helped Nicklaus learn to use a variety of elevations in his short game and unlocked his curiosity.

"Tiger Woods has maybe over one hundred different [short game] shots. Jack didn't have a lot of variety. I think I stimulated his interest and creativity."

All the pieces were now in place, but they would have been worthless without a critical leavening ingredient.

"You've got to be patient," says Nicklaus. "You've got to take your time and work at it."

It seems obvious, but to those who struggle with the game, climbing out of the abyss can't happen quickly enough. That type of anxiety can sabotage all sorts of good work and intentions.

"I mean, there's only so much mentally somebody can take in a day," he says.

Nicklaus had to wait six months in 1980 for his hard work and patience to pay dividends, but as his wife says, "He is relentlessly positive." At the age of forty, he dueled with Japan's Isao Aoki right down to the final hole at Baltusrol before not only winning the U.S. Open but breaking his own scoring record for the championship. Later that summer, he would win the PGA Championship at Oak Hill in Rochester.

———

As Nicklaus and I have driven this morning, he has offered a variety of opinions on slumps. He is not done yet.

"You have to get direction," he says. "You have to get religion in many ways. You have to believe in yourself, and you have to believe in your ability to turn things around."

There is more.

"Most people try to do something they can't. They're trying to play like Arnold Palmer when they should be playing like Mabel Palmer, meaning that they're not going to hit the ball as far as Arnold did. They're going to try to, but they really ought to try and work within their abilities."

Back now at Bob Murphy's charity event in Florida, Nicklaus eventually finds someone who thinks it's okay to admit him without the requisite paperwork, recognizing that perhaps his career body of work should serve as a kind of credential in perpetuity for entrance into any facility where flags sprout from small holes in the ground and bend in the wind. Almost by rote, he stops along the way to the tee and holds out his hand to receive the Sharpies and accommodate the hundreds of people who would probably find it laughable that anyone at a golf course might not know exactly who he is. He then steps to the tee and runs through the bag with precision and dispatch. After two months away from the game, there doesn't seem to be much *rust*, only the benefit of *rest*.

There was a time in the 1970s when, behind his back, other players derisively called Nicklaus "Carnac," after the old character on Johnny Carson's *Tonight Show* who professed to have all the answers even before the questions were asked.

But after more than two months of not touching a club, as much as he will bemoan the fact that he is an "old Nicklaus," he more often seems to be the Nicklaus of old, kind of. Maybe he's got something.

"The first thing you've got to do when you're having a problem is get away from it," he says.

I add that wisdom to the list.

Chapter 3

SCOTT VERPLANK

"If you've done it once before, then you can do it again."

In the thousands of miles I traveled in the months I spent writing this book, in the dozens of people I talked with, one question continued to pop up. Have you talked to Scott Verplank?

Everybody slumps; it doesn't matter who you are, but very few have gone through what Verplank has. You'd need a motion sickness pill to comfortably consider the arc of his career. The highs were extraordinary. The lows were unimaginable.

"It was horrific," says Bob Tway, one of Verplank's closest friends, who's known him since college. "A lot of times when you're going through a stretch like that, people don't even want to sit with you in the lunch room. They think it's contagious or something."

As a college player Scott Verplank was a star. He made All-America all four years at Oklahoma State, the last three on the first team. He won the 1984 U.S. Amateur, the oldest championship in American golf and arguably the most significant title in the amateur game. But scores of players throughout history have those types of credentials. In the past half century, only one other player accomplished what Verplank did in the summer of 1985.

"AMATEUR STUNS PRO GOLF SCENE," read one major newspaper headline on that Monday, August 5.

Verplank, who had only just completed his junior year at Stillwater, won the PGA Tour's Western Open at Butler National in Chicago over a field of seasoned pros after leading wire-to-wire. Everybody was shocked—except Verplank. "I remember going there and thinking all I want to do is play like I been playing. It was very simple."

Verplank arrived in Chicago that summer on an impressive run. In successive weeks, he'd won three of amateur golf's biggest events: the Sunnehana Amateur, the Western Amateur, and the Porter Cup. This fourth week began with a win at the Western Open's Monday pro-am, and then a round of golf at nearby Medinah, which at the time had hosted two U.S. Opens.

"Never seen the course," says Verplank. "We went over there; it was kind of cool and rainy. I remember I shot 65 and set the course record."

The following day at Butler National, Verplank shot 68 to lead one of the oldest and most venerated events in American golf. "I remember everybody was like, 'Who are you?'"

Verplank had extraordinary talent, but he also had something else that proved a great and unlikely factor in his success. Something that—when he'd first discovered it twelve years before—he could have never imagined would have been anything but a burden.

———

Scott Verplank grew up a "normal" child of Dallas in the 1960s and 1970s, which is to say he rooted hard for the locals.

"My dad had season tickets to the Cowboys," he says. "He played baseball at Texas, so we rooted for the Rangers too when they moved from Washington."

Verplank took to soccer, but when the team he played on started a vigorous national travel schedule in the summers, he chose to focus on the sport he'd spent time playing with his grandmother, Elizabeth Bybee, on visits to her home in Houston. "She played golf almost every day," he says, "so she'd take me with her."

Bybee didn't hit it very far, but she had an excellent short game and impressed its importance on her grandson. Every green he one-putted when they played together at River Oaks, she gave him a quarter. By the age of twelve, he broke par back home in Dallas. He remembers the day: "We had a soccer game in the morning, and then I went and played golf in the afternoon."

Just as Verplank recalls scoring "three or four" goals and shooting 70 in the afternoon that spring day in 1976, he also remembers the January morning two and a half years earlier when life got different in a hurry. He'd been stuck at home for a few days with what the doctor had told his mother was the flu.

"I could barely get off the couch," he says.

When he didn't get any better after a few more days, his mother took him back to the doctor's office.

"He looks at me and goes, 'Get to the hospital, now,'" recalls Verplank.

Verplank's mother loaded him in the car and rushed him to the same place where President John Kennedy was taken on November 22, 1963: the emergency room at Parkland Hospital.

"I remember getting in the back seat of my mom's car, and I thought I was having a heart attack. My heart was beating like two hundred beats a minute. I thought my heart was going to explode out of my chest. And that's the last thing I remember."

Verplank lapsed into a coma, which lasted more than a week. When he woke up, the doctors told him he had diabetes. Much of an elementary school student's care-free existence was instantly stripped away. The nurses brought an orange to his bedside and stuck it with a hypodermic needle to demonstrate what Verplank would now need to do every day. And then he was told he'd had his last ice cream cone.

"I remember saying, 'What? I can't have ice cream anymore? I'm a nine-year-old!'" says Verplank, "and they said, 'No, it'd probably be best if you didn't.' Obviously, my whole life changed."

Verplank became an introvert, the better to keep people away and discourage them from asking "messy" questions.

"I really didn't let anybody in or let anybody know that much about me," he says. "I didn't want them to think I was some sort of freak because I had to take shots and do all that."

His reticence and aloof demeanor made the perfect suit of armor to keep him protected and immersed in his own little world. As challenging as it was, the diabetes served him well as a golfer. "It made me tougher mentally than almost everybody else that I was playing against," he says, "because I had to be."

"He had to grow up in a hurry," says Tway. "Most kids are just kind of running around doing whatever, but he had to become very regimented in what he did. He was so much more mature than all the other players."

In rainy conditions that 1985 Sunday afternoon in Chicago, the twenty-one-year-old college senior-to-be beat Tour veteran Jim Thorpe on the second hole of a sudden death playoff. It was the first time in twenty-nine years an amateur had won on the PGA Tour.

"Everybody's thinking an alien had landed," he says, "I'm just doing what I know how to do."

A week later at the LaJet Amateur Classic in Abilene,

Texas, Verplank shot a final round 62 and made it five straight tournament wins before heading back to school to reap the rewards of his remarkable summer.

"Me and the quarterback," he laughs, "we were pretty big guys."

That spring, he graduated from school with a 3.5 grade average in business administration and started his life as a professional golfer. It was different. Most everybody was just as good and focused as he was. He didn't enjoy the same rabid success he had in the amateur game, but he set about establishing himself as a sturdy, dependable presence. In the spring of 1988, his first win as a pro came at the Buick Open in Michigan. He'd started dating the sister-in-law of fellow player Dillard Pruitt. He finished thirty-first on the money list. Life was good.

And then, toward the end of the 1990 season, an ominous and almost overlooked harbinger arrived: his right elbow started to ache just a little bit. Verplank dismissed it—"something always hurt," he says—but soon after he noticed he was becoming increasingly erratic from the tee and the fairway.

"And I'm like, 'That didn't feel like a bad swing. What happened there?'"

Something wasn't working the way it was supposed to. That dull ache in his right elbow was obviously becoming something more than just a "handful of Advil" problem. Still, Verplank pressed on because that was his way. He completed a decent season with four top-ten finishes, including a near miss in Boston, where he finished second to Morris Hatalsky by a single shot.

Golfers come and go on the PGA Tour. Bad seasons happen. But total cataclysmic disasters, like that which descended on Verplank the following year, don't usually befall players of his caliber. It was incomprehensible. He started in Tucson the second week of January 1991 and proceeded to miss fifteen straight cuts. The last week of June, he withdrew from Memphis and then missed six more. By year's end, the bottom line was ugly: twenty-six events, and only once—at Las Vegas in his next-to-last event of the season—did he play on the weekend.

"I learned to not really say a whole lot when he was done on Fridays," says his wife, Kim, who concedes it was probably a good thing they were young and lost in newlywed bliss. Although Scott handled it really well, she says, he understandably had his moments, like that Friday afternoon in Atlanta when he'd just missed his twelfth straight cut.

"We're walking up a hill, and he kicked this trash can, and it flipped over—and I just kept walking on. I'm going to act like I don't even know him. And I got to the top of the hill and I turned around and he was down there picking up all these ice cream boxes and putting them back in the trash can, and I'm like, 'Oh, Honey, it'll get better.'"

That season, Verplank earned the Tour's ignominious triple crown: last in driving distance, last in driving accuracy, and last in greens-in-regulation.

"The problem was, I didn't know how to quit," he says. We are sitting in the dining room at TPC Sawgrass. It is early in the week of the Players, and from a comfortable vantage point of sixteen years, it is all so much easier to understand. Diabetes, initially a burden that later gave him the interpersonal tools to withstand golf's pressure, had now turned and had started to work against him again.

"I didn't know when to take a step back and say 'Listen, I got a real problem,'" admits Verplank. "My elbow kept hurting, kept losing strength, but I've overcome stuff my whole life. I've had to since I was nine years old. So I'll be okay; I'll just overcome it."

Verplank estimates he'd lost perhaps 70 percent of the strength in that arm. The only way he realized he could finally "overcome" the problem was through surgery, which he had in November 1991.

"They scoped it [arthroscopy]," he says, "basically trying to take the easy way out. Just cut off some little spurs and see if that would relieve the pain and the weakness."

And for a little while, it did. Verplank returned to the Tour in March. But 1992 quickly started to look sadly similar to 1991, and by October it was almost a mirror image. He played thirteen events and made one cut. In August, he even missed a cut on the Nationwide Tour, golf's high-level minor league.

"It was brutal, but I never felt embarrassed," he says.

"Maybe I'm a jerk, but I don't really care that much about what other people think. I'm in my own little world. I remember being really angry and sad and confused."

By this point it was clear that whatever the arthroscopy had done, it hadn't done enough. So Verplank went to see Dr. Frank Jobe, the eminent surgeon and pioneer in orthopedic sports medicine, particularly surgery of the elbow. In 1974, Jobe, using a procedure he had developed, reconstructed the elbow of a thirty-one-year-old Los Angeles Dodgers pitcher. Tommy John surgery, as it came to be known, was a major medical breakthrough and eventually saved the careers of scores of major leaguers. But Jobe was not quite so optimistic when he first examined Verplank. "He had a thing called osteochondritis dissecans," says Jobe, "which is usually a career-ending disease. Very severe."

The cartilage in Verplank's right elbow had lost its blood supply, and the bone surrounding it was dead.

"My joint was basically falling apart," says Verplank. "It was getting soft and mushy."

So Jobe drilled a pair of holes in the bone to revascularize the area. Despite the severity of Verplank's condition, he actually felt comforted. There was a reason he had played so poorly.

"Physically, I was unfit to play like I'm used to playing," he says, "so that gave me the tiny bit of inspiration to hang on and fight it out and get through all the injury stuff and then learn how to play golf again."

It would not be easy. Verplank lost all of 1993 to rehab, but when he came back in 1994, the roller coaster started quickly chugging up the hill. He climbed from 309th on the money list to 97th. In nineteen events, he missed just five cuts and recorded his first top ten in nearly four years He was on his way.

But if Scott Verplank had learned one thing as his career moved along, it was to be wary of providence, at least when it came to his health. After improving his position again in 1995, the following year ended early and abruptly. He needed another arthroscopy—this time on his *left* elbow.

"That knocked me in the dirt more than the other deal [1992] did," he says. "I'd just fought my ass off for three years. I just came out of the hole. I just came out of the abyss, and then I just get my legs cut off."

The operation would fix his elbow, but at this point it almost wasn't about the physical issues anymore.

"You're so beat down," says his wife. "I don't know how he got through it other than he's the most stubborn, toughest person I've ever known. I would have probably given up a long time ago."

Verplank got up off the canvas yet again, and in late 1997 he went back to Q-School, which he won by six strokes. Then he started what he calls his second career. "I'm always of the attitude," he says, "that if you've done it once before, then you can do it again. If you've played well before, there's only one thing keeping you from playing well again. You."

Starting in 1998, finally healthy, Verplank took up where he'd left off almost a decade before. He has won three more events and finished an average of twenty-eighth on the money list since then, while becoming one of the most accurate ball strikers in the game. "Forget about Comeback Player of the Year," says Paul Azinger. "He should get comeback player of the century."

"I think that just shows you how tough the guy is," says Tway, "and it's why he's such a great competitor at the Ryder Cup and the Presidents Cup." Other names might be sexier, but none are more successful in team play for the United States over the past decade than Verplank. He's won ten of the fourteen matches in which he's played.

"When you talk to him, you get the sense that he's figured something out about it as an individual, that maybe we haven't figured out as a team," says one man who's participated in both competitions over the last decade. "He'd make a great captain."

It was Scott Verplank's response to physical adversity as a nine-year-old that helped him develop the attitude that made him a great player. In the end, that same determination almost ruined him. In golf, as much as you should listen to your instructor, the most important voice to hear is the voice of your body.

"If your body hurts," he says, "your mind doesn't function very well, and that's just another hurdle to overcome."

Chapter 4

DAVID DUVAL

*"I think the most precious commodity in golf that
needs to be guarded is your confidence."*

It is a hot August evening in 1999 in the canyons north-
west of Los Angeles, and David Duval is literally sitting near the top of the world—the world of golf.
With a two-shot win at the Players Championship just
five months earlier, he ascended to the game's number one
ranking, a position he held for three months before Tiger
Woods narrowly wrested it away from him in July. Later
this very week he will seize it back again.

The two players are friends but seemingly nothing
alike. Woods, with his megawatt smile, is the polyethnic
son of a military officer from southern California. Duval
is white, the son of a golf professional, and from Florida. To many he seems impassive and aloof. It is often
suggested that he wears his omnipresent mirrored wrap-
around sunglasses to hide.

But both he and Woods have come to the Sherwood
Country Club united in purpose and station. They are

here for a carnival creation precipitated by an indisput-
able reality: they are not merely the top two players in
the game—no one else is even close. So IMG, the firm
that at the time represents both players, and ABC Sports
have put together a head-to-head match between the two.
Not only a match that will be televised in prime time—a
first for golf, certainly exhibition golf—but a match that
will end up finishing under temporary stadium lighting
installed specially for the event. Nothing like this has
ever been done before. It has the feel of a rock concert, or
maybe a big-time promotion of another kind.

"It was a prize fight on the golf course," says Charley
Moore, who at the time worked for IMG representing
Duval and remembers the "tale of the tape" boxing-
style posters that were printed for the event. "It was very
circus-like."

Grown men, cigars in hand, who'd paid $550 for club-
house passes, climbed boulders and trees to get a glimpse
of the game's dynamic duo. On television, the match produced a 6.5 rating, which exceeded the viewership guaranteed to sponsors—a somewhat rare occurrence in the
industry's contemporary landscape.

"I'm a golf star," Duval had told Clifton Brown of the
New York Times earlier that year, "but he's a star."

Woods, who would go on to win the match on the seventeenth hole, was indeed the game's top attraction, but
Duval was in the conversation. After the match that night,
he and his friends ended up at Wayne Gretzky's nearby

house, hanging out with a crew of some twenty-five athletes and Hollywood celebrities until about three in the morning. Gretzky's wife, the actress Janet Jones, cooked everyone breakfast. It was a good time, but such a long time ago, longer even than years seem to be able to measure.

In the blink of an eye, it is nine years later, and things are considerably different.

Duval and I are sitting in the back of the locker room at the Honda Classic in Palm Beach Gardens, Florida. It is the first week of March 2008, and he is now the world's 772nd-ranked player. He hasn't had a top-ten finish in nearly five and a half years. As we sit talking he has yet to make a cut in five starts. He won't make it to the weekend until the year is halfway done, when he finishes tied for 60th in Memphis.

"Maybe I'm one of the few players who play this game for a living," Duval had told Jeff Rude of *Golfweek* magazine, "who truly knows what great golf is about, and what awful golf is about too." In fact, never in the game's contemporary history has a player experienced such wild swings in fortune and accomplishment. When Duval was good, he was at times untouchable, like that Sunday in 1999 at the Bob Hope Chrysler Classic. He shot 59—only the third player in PGA Tour history to record a score so low. It was his second win in just two starts that season. All told, he won four times in his first eight starts and never finished worse than 18th during the stretch. It was a common point of discussion back then: was he—not Woods—the best player in the world?

"I have told everybody before: I certainly want to be considered that at some point in my career," he said after his 59 at the Hope, "and if I am considered that now, I am flattered and excited, but I still have to keep trying to improve. Got to keep trying to get better and try to add some U.S. Opens and PGAs and such to my resume."

But just a few years later, the thought of Duval even contending in a major, let alone making the cut, would have been far-fetched. As good as he was during that run in 1999, he had become just as lost by 2005.

After withdrawing from the first event of the year in San Diego that season, he missed sixteen straight cuts. In twenty events, he played once on the weekend and earned a total of $7,630. All those missed cuts meant that Duval hadn't played enough to meet the minimum number of rounds to be ranked officially in the Tour's various statistical categories, but if he had, he would have been last in scoring, last in greens-in-regulation, last in driving accuracy, and 183rd (out of 202) in putting. It was as woeful a season as anyone—let alone a former number one player—has ever had.

"I remember watching him hit shots," says seven-time PGA Tour winner Peter Jacobsen, "where a tee ball would go forty yards to the right, and then the next one would go forty yards to the left."

In the time since, things got better—and then again, just as bad.

"Do you think you could ever be what you were?" I ask him.

"Do you mean number one? That would be very hard," he says, acknowledging his old friend's remarkable skill and accomplishment.

"I don't know if anybody'll be number one while Tiger's playing, frankly. From top to bottom, his golf game is so much more complete than anybody else's has ever been. I don't mean it in a disrespectful or disparaging way, but I'm trying to guess how many majors Jack [Nicklaus] would have won had he been competing against Tiger, and I think it would have been less than ten."

He pauses for a moment, maybe to reflect on the gravity of what he's just said. Then he clarifies further: "I'd say six."

We sit for a moment quietly, and then Duval drifts back to my original question.

"But I think I could be the player I once was," he says. "Yes. I don't think you have to bust your ass. I mean, I never particularly busted my ass working—practicing and playing. I did the things I needed to do and spent a ton of time hitting wedges."

Despite the horrific stretch he's endured over the past few years, Duval is actually hopeful, even though recent results appear to contradict any reason for optimism.

"I think I'm certainly at this point on the cusp of something," he says. "I should be a Ryder Cup player for the U.S. I don't think there's twelve players better than me."

"I suppose you've got to have confidence," I suggest.

"The thing I feel like I learned the most through anything," he says, "is that the most precious commodity in golf that needs to be guarded is your confidence. By far, you've got to protect it at all costs. Losing friends, losing whatever—you've got to protect your confidence."

Duval's path into the golf abyss can be traced to a handful of very identifiable mileposts, and it began with something that haunts more than a few people who play this game: back pain. The problem actually started with his natural but somewhat unusual anatomy.

"I'm a little over six foot tall," he says, "and I have a twenty-nine-inch inseam." By comparison, I'm six inches shorter than Duval, and my inseam is an inch longer. The translation: Duval's back is about four inches longer than average for his height. He was also hyperflexible. So when he sprained his lower back in the spring of 2000, it was an especially big and important moving part of his golfing mechanism.

Still, he was able to play effectively at first. He had nine top-ten finishes on the PGA Tour in 2000, and the following year, after finishing finished second at the Masters, he won the biggest prize he'd yet to collect: the British Open at Royal Lytham and St. Annes. But even at his brightest moment, there were telltale signs of trouble.

"I won seventeen or eighteen times as a pro," he says,

"and that was by far the worst I ever hit a golf ball in a tournament I won."

The win at Lytham also exposed another problem, this one not physical but mental, and perhaps more damaging. That Sunday night after winning the championship, Duval fulfilled the numerous media obligations and was immediately whisked off to a luxury-outfitted 737 chartered by the organizers of the Canadian Skins game, which was being played the following week.

"Vijay [Singh], Mike [Weir], and a bunch of family members were on the plane," remembers Moore. "After awhile, everybody else fell asleep, and David and I were drinking champagne from the Claret Jug. I remember as we were landing, the sun was coming up, and we were pulling into Toronto and David says to me: 'I would have thought it would feel better than this.'"

Duval termed it his "existentialist moment."

"I started to think: 'That's it? That's all there is?'" he recalls.

The thing he'd been chasing for so long, since his days as a child following around his father the club pro, since his days at Georgia Tech as one of only a handful of young men to have ever been chosen first team All-America four consecutive years—supremacy in golf—left him feeling strangely unfulfilled. He had poured himself relentlessly into the game for as long as he could remember, and though he didn't realize it at the time, there was a tremendous cost.

"I think the sacrifices have to come from somewhere," he says. "The time has to come from somewhere, and for me I was in a bad spot personally for several years, so maybe that's also what helped me focus golf-wise so much."

At a time in his life when he should have been happiest, Duval was confused and melancholy. He soon parted with his long-time fiancée and started to monkey around with some changes in his golf game that would allow him to swing pain-free.

"When you have a bad hip, or a bad knee, or a bad back, or a bad neck," says Jacobsen, who in the past couple of years has had a knee and a hip replaced, as well as back surgery, "not only do you consciously swing to avoid the pain, but subconsciously your brain's not going to let your body hurt, whether you're walking up the stairs, sitting down, or hitting a driver, so you develop compensations which result in bad habits, which result in your golf ball going sideways. David had one of the best swings maybe in the history of the game, and when his back hurt him he started swinging more upright. He stopped turning his body around, and he started turning his arms in front of his body."

His swing went from flat to upright. He started "lifting and waving" the club. "Oh," he says, cringing at the memory; "it was just awful." By 2002, Duval had added injuries to his shoulder and wrist to his balky back. On top of it all, the following season he got vertigo.

"It was kind of like the perfect storm," says Moore. "The guy just couldn't buy a break."

His physical frailties, combined with his disillusionment and unhappiness, all amounted to a toxic alchemy. The slump began in earnest the following year as he slid all the way from 80th to 212th on the PGA Tour's money list. It was his worst year to date. But amidst the professional ineffectiveness came a personal epiphany. The first week in August 2002, while playing in the International in Denver, Duval met a divorcée named Susie Persichitte. In an instant, his life was no longer empty, and golf didn't seem that important anymore.

Just as Arnold Palmer had once done, Duval simply put down the clubs and took a break. But while Palmer's sabbatical lasted five weeks, Duval's was *eight months*. He married and became a stepfather of Persichitte's three children. This solitary figure, who'd seen his family start to come apart at the seams at age nine when his older brother, Brent, died of aplastic anemia despite a bone marrow transplant from David, this boy whose parents split up a few years later, all of a sudden was knee-deep in the middle of something he'd really never had—a family.

"I'm learning to be a husband, learning to be a father, learning to be a son again," he said at the time. "I feel like in Denver with my wife and the family out there that I've finally found home."

More balanced and happy, Duval decided he was ready to play golf again. But of all the places for reentry he chose the one at which he could incinerate before he might even have a chance to splash down: the most difficult event of the year, the U.S. Open.

"The life out on this Tour and in professional golf is long, it's hard, and it's lonely," he told a packed press room the day before the championship started that year at Shinnecock Hills. "I've been doing this for a long, long time, and in some sense I haven't missed it. I haven't missed being away, but I just wanted to play this week. The U.S. Open is a very hard thing for me to miss, and I was anxious for my wife and family to see me and see what I do, to see the atmosphere of golf."

Playing early on Thursday morning, he birdied Shinnecock's dogleg right, par-four first hole; and for a moment, golf's lost soul seemed to have found himself and was actually leading the Open. But reality restored itself not long after. Duval went on to shoot rounds of 83 and 82—25 over par, and the second to worst score in the entire field.

———

Golf-wise, not much changed over the next four years. As we sit talking in the locker room in Florida, Duval has made the cut in only nineteen of the sixty-five events he's played since coming back at Shinnecock, but he is unmistakably happy.

"Yeah," he says, "I found my place, if you will. I think that for a long, long time I sought greatness—you know, identity through golf."

He doesn't any longer. He sees himself as a husband, and stepfather, and now a parent (he and Susie have two kids together). Others might snicker behind his back when they hear him say that he's right around the corner from playing well, but he won't allow it to chip away at the most important thing he needs to get back: confidence. "You know, it's kind of a catch-22 of American society. They love their studs and heroes, but they hate cocky people."

Duval's self-belief serves him well. A few months after we chatted in the locker room in Florida, that cusp he felt he was sitting on became more apparent. He challenged for the lead through the first 36 holes at the British Open before eventually finishing tied for 39th—mostly because of a disastrous third round that was played in near gale-force winds and started with a triple bogey.

"I played beautifully," Duval recalls thinking after the round. "I just shot 83 and I mis-hit three, maybe four golf shots."

But it was hardly an awakening for Duval, who beat, among others, Vijay Singh, Sergio Garcia, Zach Johnson, and Colin Montgomerie.

"That week sums up the battle I have internally," says Duval. "I expect so much from myself. Certainly there are times when I wonder: can I do this? But in my soul, I expect true excellence. I had a rough test the front nine on Saturday: I shot 10 over par. You pull that out, and I'm right there."

"The restoration project," he had told me a few months earlier, "it's 97 percent complete mechanically. I'm very much towards the end of that. I just have to work on my head a little bit. Physically, I'm playing well enough to compete on Tour to win. I'm not firing on all cylinders necessarily, but it's awful close and I'm talented enough— that's enough. Just a matter of getting my head straight and getting some confidence.

"The most enjoyment I ever got out of playing was controlling the golf ball—you know, some little round sphere with dimples in it—up through the air, and that's what I got the most pleasure out of, every bit as much as winning a golf tournament, and I totally lost that. And I'm totally enjoying hitting the ball and controlling it again."

With his distant and unemotional demeanor, there was a time it might have seemed hard to root for David Duval. Now he seems hard to root against. "Golf *is* like life," former President George H. W. Bush has noted. It tells you a lot about a person. Golf is also like life in that its stories don't always have happy endings, but Duval is confident he is heading in the right direction.

"Take this for what it's worth," he tells me. "It'll all come to fruition before your book is published."

Duval's game is a work in progress, but in life he seems to have found his happy ending.

Chapter 5

DAN JANSEN

"Get this golf ball right here, right now with all my energy. Usually, when I hit a bad one, I know right away that somewhere, my mind was wandering . . . I wasn't all in."

It is a warm Sunday afternoon in February at the PGA National Resort and Spa in Palm Beach Gardens, Florida and although the sun is still lazily drifting toward the horizon, the stars are already out. The actor and comedian Cheech Marin poses for pictures with passersby in the lobby, while over on a barstool, former New York Giants running back and Super Bowl XXV MVP Otis "O.J." Anderson holds court. Boris Becker is here, and so is Lawrence Taylor. They have all gathered for a charity golf outing the following day hosted by Tico Torez, not only the drummer for the rock band Bon Jovi but a hardcore golf freak as well.

Out on the balcony overlooking the golf course, Dan Jansen sits quietly sipping a beer. At 197 pounds, he is virtually the same weight as when he won his Olympic speed skating gold medal in Norway in 1994, but the weight is redistributed. Then, he needed specially tailored pants to cover his massive thighs. Now, the muscle seems to have migrated northward as a pitiable golf shirt fights a losing battle to cover his bulging arms. We are talking golf, and he is sounding like Yogi Berra. "I didn't realize that I wasn't any good," he laughs, "until I started to get better."

No one asks for an autograph. No one interrupts his conversation, which is both fine and odd. Twenty years ago, almost to the day, he was the biggest story in sports and perhaps something more.

Dan Jansen grew up in West Allis, Wisconsin, the youngest of nine children, totally obsessed with anything his older siblings wanted to do. Most times that meant sports.

"I grew up believing that because I was the youngest of so many, I could do anything as well as they could," he says. Golf was a popular choice in the Jansen house because, as Dan says, his dad was a "golf nut." By age nine, DJ was playing. By high school, he was actually on the golf team, but that is something of a misleading credential.

"Whoever tried out pretty much played, because there weren't many guys that were going to do it," he says. "Most of the tournaments were nine holes. We shot in the 40 to 45 range."

The already short Wisconsin golf season was truncated even further when Jansen started to develop as a speed skater. But after he graduated from high school, skating actually provided the perfect window for golf. The World Cup season ended in March, and summer training didn't resume until May.

"It was a good relief to get away from skating, or thinking about training," says Jansen, who once told me his training regimen was so savage that when he showered at night, he had to use a chair because he was too tired to stand.

So, with limited time to play or practice, and never having taken a lesson, Jansen's game idled at "about a 10 handicap" throughout his competitive speed skating career. The son of a policeman who grew up playing county courses for $1.50 greens fees, after retirement he would very soon come to understand golf's addictive magnetism and its merciless and unpredictable ups and downs. But he felt sure that any adversity he might find in golf would be manageable. How could it possibly compare to the last six years of his life?

During those years, Jansen was the dominant sprint speed skater of his time. He won forty-six World Cup races—the third best of all time—and broke eight world records. His specialty was the 500 meters, where he was nearly unbeatable. "That race," he says, "that was my baby."

Actually, according to Johan Van den Heuvel, a Dutch

speed skating journalist and statistician who has covered the sport since 1968, Jansen wasn't just the best of his time at the 500. "At the time, he was the best that ever was."

He first became the object of public attention on Valentine's Day in 1988. Jansen was favored to win the 500 meters at the Calgary Olympics, but at six o'clock that morning, there was a knock at his door. He was called to the phone to speak with his older sister Jane, stricken with leukemia, who lay dying in a Wisconsin hospital. Jansen recounts the call in his autobiography *Full Circle:* "I don't remember exactly what I said, but I told her I loved her and that I was going to win the race that night for her, even though I didn't believe it myself. There was not much else to say. My sister was dying and I was helpless, so far away from her. I couldn't hear a sound, not even the whir of the respirator she was hooked up to. Later, Diane and Joanne [his sisters] told me they were positive Jane had heard me, because she breathed on her own while I was talking. I hope so. I really hope so."

Five hours later, Jansen called his brother Jim, who told him their sister had passed away. Dan was both devastated and confused. How could he skate? How could he not? At five o'clock that evening, he took to the ice to fulfill the promise he had made to his late sister. He says he felt "wobbly." Later, he would write in his race journal: "When I got to the line, I don't remember what I was thinking, but I know that when the starter said 'ready,' I wasn't."

Jansen false started, a rarity for him. On the restart, he skated the first 100 meters in 9.9 seconds—a performance he termed "hideous." And then, two strides into the first turn, he wiped out.

"What a day!" he wrote in his journal. "Good night, Jane. Rest in peace."

Jansen thought he had been living in his own little world, but he soon found out that others had been peering over the hedge. The luge teams sent flowers. The hockey team sent cards. Thousands of people from his hometown signed a ninety-six-foot-long banner that read DAN, BE STRONG! KEEP THE FAITH! WISCONSIN IS WITH YOU ALL THE WAY.

The 1,000 meters was four days later, and with the world now enthralled with this tragic tale, Jansen publicly dedicated the race to his sister. And then, after leading for 800 meters, he fell again.

His life had officially become a saga. Four years later in Albertville, France, he would try again. In a way, Jansen was fortunate this time around because this was the Olympic Games of Tonya Harding and Nancy Kerrigan, so his story was somewhat overshadowed. But in both races, he failed again, though not so spectacularly. In the 500, rain created an unfavorable ice condition for Jansen's style of skating, and he missed a bronze medal by 0.16 seconds. Still thunderstruck by his bad fortune, three days later he skated poorly in the 1,000 and finished 26th. "I just mentally wasn't there."

In his autobiography, he marveled at the misperception one week can create: "I'm not bragging, but merely stating a fact when I say that, regardless of my Olympic performances, I was destined to go down as one of the greatest speed skaters in history, maybe the greatest in the 500 meters. But to millions of other casual fans, I was either a choker, an Olympic klutz, or, at best, the all-time Heartbreak Kid . . . I bet half the Olympic audience wondered if I ever actually remained upright on a pair of skates."

With the Winter Olympics shifted to alternate every two years with the Summer Games, Jansen would have one last chance in 1994. Somehow, in the 500, he briefly lost his footing, and the misstep cost him a medal. He finished eighth.

Jansen remembers sitting down after the race and his coach Peter Mueller coming over to console him. Mueller mentioned something about the 1,000 and Jansen said, "I don't even want to skate the 1,000. This could not have possibly happened again. There's no way this could have happened."

All that remained in an Olympic career that had started with such promise—a fourth-place finish in the 500 meters in Sarajevo ten years earlier as the team's youngest skater—now came down to one race: the 1,000 meters.

At the urging of a sponsor, Jansen had been working with a sports psychologist, Dr. Jim Loehr, who had advised several elite athletes, including golfer Mark O'Meara.

Jansen and Loehr had worked hard on trying *not* to think about two things: his sister Jane and falling, a task made harder in that those were generally the first two topics most journalists wanted to talk to him about.

"But the second thing we worked on," says Jansen, "was getting me to like the 1,000 meters, because I truly, deep down, didn't like the race. I wasn't that good in it. I was capable physically, but mentally I wasn't."

On February 18, 1994, Jansen went out and confounded not only himself but many experts as well. After slipping in the third to last turn, he righted himself and finally delivered on the promise he had made to his sister six years earlier. Jansen won the gold medal in world record time. He'd convinced himself that he "liked" the 1,000. He took a call from the president, carried the American flag in the closing ceremony, and then came home to try and catch up on all the things he had put aside while he'd poured himself into skating.

Out on the lobby balcony overlooking the PGA National almost exactly fourteen years later, Jansen, forever the speed skater, is explaining why he came home and took up golf with a passion.

"You know," he says, "I like team sports, and I have no trouble playing, but I just gravitated a little more towards the solitary stuff. I'm on my own out here [the golf course], and whatever I put into this, I get out of it. Not that I don't like to rely on other people, I just like to rely on myself. I think golf is that way."

As we sit talking, Jansen's wife stops by. I have always joked with them that he brought golf obsession to a new level: he married his pro.

"People give him such a hard time," says Karen Palacios-Jansen, the LPGA's 2008 Teacher of the Year. "They'll say 'oh, you're married to a pro, you must get lessons all the time,' and he'll say 'yeah, but I'm not that good.'"

A few years after he retired from competition, Jansen was going through a divorce and went to Orlando to spend some time with Loehr. The two played golf, and when Jansen stopped by the Ledbetter Academy for a lesson, Palacios was assigned as his instructor. They struck up a friendship and four years later were married. The two now live in Charlotte, North Carolina, and Jansen has gotten his handicap down to a 2.4 index. He is a frequent participant in celebrity events and takes the game very seriously.

"It's been discouraging," he says. "Look, I'm already over forty. I'm never going to be great at the game, but I do think I have the potential to be a lot better than I am."

Jansen's problem is that he's haunted. Once he was "the best" at something, and what came with that was an awareness.

"I know what the gap is," he says. "I know what the gap is between the best and mediocrity, and it's huge. The best golfers out there—the pros—no matter what my level is, I'm a complete hack to them, and I have trouble getting that out of my mind."

Skating "scarred" him in another way, too. "Being a sprinter," he says, "one slip and that's it, and it's hard because that's my mentality."

In golf, that can be ruinous thinking.

"Why even continue if you're on the third hole and you make double or triple bogey? Now, I try really hard to say: 'That's done. There's nothing you can do about it.' It used to bother me for three holes."

As a skater Jansen was highly technical. As a golfer he operates in a similar fashion. But, oddly, the strength of his game as a skater—focus and positive productive thinking—is the weakest part of his game as a golfer, so he's gone back to Loehr, who has tried to get him to think about being in the moment, or what he calls energy management.

"You can give energy to negative stuff, and that gives it life," says Jansen. "So now, when I'm over the ball, I've been really good at getting the 'right here, right now.' Get this golf ball right here, right now with all my energy. Usually, when I hit a bad one, I know right away that somewhere, my mind was wandering . . . I wasn't all in."

Like many ex-athletes, Jansen is a tortured soul when it comes to golf. At home, he and his wife play about four times a week. He pushes himself hard and has enormous expectations.

"I know nothing about skating," says his wife, " but apparently skating and golf are very similar because in skating you have to be technically correct, and Dan was the Nick Faldo or Tiger Woods of skating. People used to watch his films to learn to skate better. And I'm always showing him video of other players, and I think that's what intrigues him—you know, 'Why can't I do it?'"

For a man who faced such profound adversity in his personal and athletic life, you'd figure the vagaries that golf presents would be no big deal. But the Olympic hero is like so many of us: the game owns him.

"You spend so many hours lying in bed thinking about this damn game for some reason," he says, "and it drives you nuts!"

Jansen feels that Loehr's "here and now" approach may be the concept which finally permits him to reach his potential, and maybe he's right. A month later, while training for a marathon he plans to run to raise money for leukemia research—a race he eventually completes in three hours and twenty minutes—he sends me an e-mail: "Had to let you know, I shot my first 69 today. Kind of came out of nowhere. Been very mediocre the last couple of weeks and today was just a great day!"

Chapter 6

JUSTIN ROSE

*"You have to invest in your mind. It's a muscle and
it needs to be trained. You don't just become mentally strong.
It doesn't just happen."*

I've been to at least fifty major championships in the time I've covered golf. Every single one had moments of drama and more than a handful of reasons why it should be remembered glowingly in the history books. But among the forest of accomplishments and legendary winners, I can't help thinking back on one in particular, which history might overlook as perhaps ordinary. In my mind, it was anything but.

Royal Birkdale is, in a sense, the stepchild of the British Open rota. It didn't receive its "Royal" designation until 1951. You won't hear people fall to pieces over its beauty the way they do for Turnberry. It doesn't claim the long history of St. Andrews, the prestige of Muirfield, or the brutality of Carnoustie. But ask a golf historian about Royal Birkdale, and there's a wealth of significant happenings to remember. Of the five British Opens that

Peter Thomson and Tom Watson each won, Birkdale was the site of the former's first and the latter's last. Arnold Palmer, Lee Trevino, and Johnny Miller all won the Claret Jug there, and Birkdale has hosted the Ryder Cup and the Walker Cup as well.

When the Open arrived at Birkdale in 1998, Tiger Woods had won one major championship, the 1997 Masters. It was actually his good friend Mark O'Meara who'd made big news in April of 1998 by becoming the oldest first-time winner of the Masters at age forty-one. As the British Open started that year I walked a practice round with O'Meara and noted that the greens appeared slow.

"You think so?" he asked me as we walked up the 18th fairway.

O'Meara handed me his putter as we arrived at the green and said the only way I'd really know was if I tried it for myself. So there, in front of a few thousand people—this was the Masters champion playing along-side his friend Woods—I got to live out a little piece of a fantasy:

And here we are at the final hole of the British Open. Roberts needs this twenty-footer to win the title. . .

As I recall, I left the putt short, but not embarrassingly so.

Overall, the week had an unusual dimension because of the presence of Ian Baker-Finch, who'd returned to the British Open for the first time since retiring from competitive golf. Baker-Finch had won the Open at Birkdale seven years earlier, and then not long afterward had spiraled down into a debilitating slump that drove him out of all but country club golf. At the 1998 Open, he worked for ESPN as a commentator, and it was an emotional week. The two of us sat next to each other on "Sports-Center" segments, and the affable Australian was entirely candid about the bittersweet emotions of returning to the site of his greatest triumph—but with a microphone in his hand instead of a golf club.

But the thing I remember most about that week is the thing I missed.

I was standing in back of the grandstand on the 18th hole speaking with Sir Michael Bonallack, at the time the secretary (boss) of the Royal and Ancient Golf Club of St. Andrews—the group that conducts the Open—when a roar shook the earth. It is without a doubt the loudest eruption of cheering I've ever heard at a golf course. Bonallack and I scrambled around the corner and saw not a single person seated or silent. A seventeen-year old English amateur named Justin Rose had pulled off a near-impossible feat. Lying two in the tall grass to the left of the green, Rose looked as if he'd be lucky just to make it out of the knee-high rough. But he did that, and then some. Rose pitched in for birdie, and the crowd was delirious.

"If I look back and watch it," he says, "I actually look a bit sheepish. I think I almost pulled my hat over my face. It was like: 'What have I done?' I mean it was a one in a thousand shot—really, it was."

One in a thousand.

Before the week started, that would have probably been an understatement of the odds that Rose could have even made the cut, let alone be a factor. But, possessed of some preternatural calm, he continued day after day to *not* go away. Bernhard Langer, Seve Ballesteros, and Tom Lehman, all major champions, missed the cut, but there was Rose on Saturday, alone in fifth position, just three strokes out of the lead. Already giddy with the emergence of a new young football star named Michael Owen, England now became positively overwhelmed with its sporting good fortune. (Earlier that summer, the eighteen-year-old Owen became the youngest player ever from his country to score a goal in the World Cup.)

"Suddenly there was the prospect of two fairly fresh-faced, genuine young sporting heroes emerging in the sporting complex in the same time," said John Hopkins of the *London Times*, "So to have Justin coming along after Michael Owen meant that excitement was far greater."

"I had the intelligence, golfing-wise, to realize there was no pressure on me, and that nobody expected anything of me," says Rose. "You know, they were all very excited about my position, but I kind of knew they were expecting me to shoot 80. It's kind of what kids do in that sort of situation. So I just went out there and free-wheeled it. I remember standing over the ball all week and thinking: it doesn't matter where I hit the ball because I'm going to get it up and down. So let's get on with it. My short game was so good that week."

O'Meara won the championship after topping Brian Watts in a playoff, but Rose might have been just as big a story. With a 66 on Sunday (the same final round score as Woods), improbably, he finished tied for fourth—the best result by an amateur in a major since Jack Nicklaus placed the same at the U.S. Open thirty-seven years earlier. And with his miraculous closing brush stroke, nothing was ever the same again.

It started the next day when he and his dad caught a flight from Manchester back to London. As the plane headed southeast toward Heathrow airport, a voice came over the public address system and announced that they would soon be landing at "Heath-*ROSE*."

"Did I just hear that right?" wondered an incredulous Rose.

It was only the start. The airport arrival hall was jammed with well-wishers, cameras, and journalists. His street at home was lined with television trucks.

"There were reporters walking around my village just interviewing random people," says Rose, "stopping people and asking, 'Do you know Justin?'"

The woman who cut his hair was questioned. A couple of girls who just happened to be standing next to him in a school picture were tracked down. "It was crazy," he says.

That Monday, in the midst of it all, Rose turned professional and accepted an invitation to play three days later in the Dutch Open, where the madness continued.

"If I look back on it now," he says, "I was probably asked to do a lot more that week than was probably reasonable."

Rose was exploited and didn't really have a shot at playing well, but it wasn't only the demands on his time. In one week's time he had gone from an amateur from whom nobody expected much to a professional whom people wanted to see make magic again—and quickly.

"I turned up to the golf course on the first round Thursday—I'm playing in the afternoon—and the leaderboard has "ROSE" on it at the top with no numbers yet. I'm like, 'What's going on?'"

In his first round as a professional, Rose shot 77, but the next day he rebounded nicely with 65. Then, though, came an odd twist of fate that might have changed his life. The last player in the last group birdied the last hole, moving the score necessary to play on the weekend from even par—Rose's score—to minus one.

Rose missed the cut.

"One guy, one putt, whatever," he says.

One missed cut for a professional is not a disaster. Other than Tiger Woods, it happens to everyone. But when you are Justin Rose, on the heels of the previous week's events at the British Open, it raises an eye. And when it turns out to be the first of many, it is the start of a legend.

Rose went the following week to play in Sweden, and again came up short. There was nowhere to hide. Everyone wanted to see him, and when he couldn't produce, it started to affect the way he looked at the task. Instead of doing what had made him successful—thinking only about the most important shot, the one he was about to play—he started thinking about making cuts.

"You know, momentum can work both directions really," he says, "and the momentum started to snowball in the wrong direction, and before you know it, how the hell do you ever make a cut?"

For a long time, he didn't. The lad who not long before had been the toast of the game now appeared to have a game that was toast. The pressure, he says, became excruciating.

"Every time I got close to making the cut—I'm talking about the sixteenth, seventeenth, eighteenth, and nineteenth attempts—I'd be out there, and as soon as I had a few holes to go and had a chance, the cameras would come out of the trees. Suddenly people would get wind of the fact that I might make my first cut, and the crowds would triple.

"It was terrible. And then I'd fail in front of everybody, and then it'd be even tougher. The pressure of that is way tougher than the pressure of actually trying to win a tournament."

And with each missed cut came another handful of suggestions from people who thought they could help him.

"Everyone comes out of the woodwork," he says.

At one point he tried something called NLP, or neuro-linguistic programming, where you tap yourself on certain parts of your body to stimulate your brain to think certain things. "This guy wanted me to tap the top of my lip before hitting a putt. I'm like, 'Listen, there's not a chance on this earth I'm going to be on the golf course, on camera, doing that.'"

How had he ever gotten to this desperate point? Golf was a job. It used to be nothing but fun.

Justin Rose started playing golf at as early an age as you'd imagine is possible. In a dresser drawer somewhere he knows there are pictures of him at home in South Africa swinging his plastic clubs at age one. His mom bought them so he could entertain himself.

"They were just toys to start with," he says. "Apparently, I wouldn't leave them alone. I'd just be out in the garden for hours and hours and hours.'

Thinking that England would be a better place to raise their children, the Rose family moved, and by the time Justin was five, he was tagging along with his father to the local course, Hartley Wintney. Ken Rose saw that his son had some aptitude and seemed to love the game, but he didn't want to push it on the child.

"If I broke 70 for nine holes," says Rose, "he'd buy me a train set or something. Just little things to keep me interested, and keep me enjoying it, and you know . . . just dangle a carrot."

Ken Rose was a self-made seven handicap. Whatever he taught his son, he learned from magazines. The idea was to keep it very simple, and it worked.

"I guess from the mental perspective, he knew me better than anybody," says Justin, " and really helped me, I guess, develop as a golfer faster than my peers."

At the age of twelve he finished 7th in the English Under-Sixteen Championships, with eye-opening scores of 75, 75, 74, and 74. By age fourteen he was a plus-one handicap and became the youngest player ever to make it through to the final stage of qualifying for the British Open. That summer, he won both the English Under-Sixteen *and* Under-Eighteen Championships. He was a genuine phenom.

Then, at sixteen years of age, Rose left school.

"I knew what I was going to do," he says, "and I had great support from my parents."

Rose says there had been a point in his young teens when he didn't think he wanted to play golf—when he just wanted to hang out with his friends down at the park, kick a soccer ball around, and "just be a bit of a delinquent." But his father gently steered him back to the game.

"I had an amazing upbringing," he says. "I seem to remember it always being my decision, but kind of realizing that I should dedicate myself to this a little bit. Some kids maybe would have rebelled against it and not wanted to do it, but I think he [dad] must have done it right because I always wanted him around.

"When I first turned pro, I was seventeen, and I obviously got off to a terrible start in my pro career," and at the time he was criticized for being too involved. "But in essence, I didn't have anybody else I could relate to out there. The next youngest guy was six years older than me, so I was way out of my depth socially."

Along with the expectation and the pressure, a large part of Rose's struggles that first year as a pro were in fact about his social discomfort. He was a kid.

"The hard thing about being a pro golfer is the lifestyle," he says, "and I just wasn't prepared or ready for it. I think when you're out of your comfort zone, you tend not to play well."

Once celebrated as the next great thing, he was—as his streak of missed cuts continued through 1998 and into 1999—introduced to the scorn of the disappointed media. He was, as one paper said, "The classic hero to zero so ingrained in the British sporting psyche."

It is ten years after Birkdale, and Rose and I are sitting in the clubhouse having breakfast at Lake Nona, a posh gated development in Orlando where several of the world's best players have lived over the years. His streak of missed cuts came to a halt when he was twenty-one, back in 1999 at the European Grand Prix near Newcastle. Rose had gone eleven months on the European Tour and in equivalent events worldwide without playing on the weekend, and when his moment of triumph finally came, it was hardly worth celebrating. He made the cut "on the number" and then the next day was timed for slow play, shot 82, and eventually finished 75th. "I thought: making the cut isn't all it's cracked up to be, you know?"

But making a cut *was* crucial, not only because by doing so you actually give yourself a chance to win a tournament, but because, in this case, of the timing. It was three weeks before the 1999 British Open at Carnoustie.

"I just couldn't bear the thought of not having made a cut since turning pro for a whole year and then turning back [up] at the Open."

That week at Birkdale had been the best thing that had ever happened in his life—and the worst, especially as he had trudged through the misery of the ensuing year.

"I thought that was the most distracting thing for me," he says. "I said, 'Okay, if that never happened, who am I?'"

Rose reminded himself that he had been the youngest Walker Cup player ever at age seventeen in 1997, with a "trophy cabinet that was overflowing" and the certainty that "I can play this game." That, in part, was how he was able to move ahead. But his hindsight is vivid and unequivocal. Turning professional the day after Birkdale and subjecting himself to the withering appraisal of a sometimes carnivorous sports media and the unrealistic expectations of the public at large was a huge mistake. It damaged not only his confidence but something just as valuable.

"I think the learning phase is so important and needs to be protected as well," he says, "and I think to this point in my career, the damage that was done initially is a long hard road to get over, and will I actually get over it 100 percent? You never know."

By most any measure, Rose is an extraordinarily successful golfer. As we sat talking that June morning, he was the world's 6th ranked player. He had just returned from Jack Nicklaus's Memorial Tournament, where he'd finished tied for 2nd. The previous year, he was the number one player on the European Tour's Order of Merit—the very same place where he couldn't make a cut eight years earlier.

Initially, after making that first cut back in 1999, it had taken Rose a few years to polish some swing mechanics and get comfortable with the life of professional golf. But he looks back fondly on those days because he was progressing, now somewhat out of the spotlight. He was also spending time with his father, who would occasionally caddy for him, as he did at the European Tour's Qualifying Tournament in the fall of 1999.

"I had like a 45-foot putt on the last hole, and I distinctly remember him saying, 'Let's make this the last putt you ever hit at Tour School'—and I rolled it in. It was a really cool moment."

Rose finished 4th and got his card. That putt didn't turn out to be his last ever at Q-School—he had to go back at the end of the next season—but 2000 was a different experience. He no longer felt like a little boy with his nose pressed up against the glass.

"I began to feel part of the Tour. I was making cuts, and I had some friends. I was on my way. The journey had begun."

The big breakthrough came in 2002, when he was twenty-two. He won four tournaments on three continents, but again, it was both the best and the worst of times, because just as Rose was starting to come into his own, his father was diagnosed with leukemia at age fifty-seven. Ken Rose had borne the brunt of the criticism when his son turned professional and then had struggled. In some quarters he was looked upon as the ultimate Little League parent who couldn't leave his child alone.

"As soon as Dad heard that criticism," Rose told Hopkins of the *London Times* in October 2002, "he said, 'Right, go out there on your own and see how you feel.' I did, and I decided, no, I felt much more comfortable with my dad on hand to help me with my golf swing, to help me out with whatever I needed. People didn't understand this."

On the heels of Justin Rose's most successful season yet—the culmination of all their work together—Ken Rose passed away in September of that year.

"I feel like he's missed out on a lot of things I'm achieving, and I'd love to be sharing stuff with him, but I don't feel bitter that I've lost him," says Rose, "because I feel like I got so much from him. Our relationship was quality, not quantity. It was brutally hard for a year or two, but I look at it now that I'm actually grateful and thankful for the relationship we had."

That Ken Rose should pass away at almost the same time as his son ascended to the most elite level of the professional game is a powerful lesson for Justin Rose, and it's not just a coincidence. De-emphasizing the importance of golf is sometimes the most effective way to get better.

"I won four times in 2002 out of nowhere, really. My game was getting better and all, but all of a sudden, I became this different player. My dad was literally on his deathbed for those few months that I won four times. I kind of knew that it was looking bleak, and suddenly that was the most important thing in my life—my dad." At the same time Rose met and started dating Kate Phillips, whom he would marry at the end of 2006.

"So I had these two really powerful things going on off the course, and they just put golf a bit more in perspective. For me, when golf becomes too important, generally I don't play well."

The pinnacle of Rose's success thus far has been the 2007 season, when he finished in the top twelve of all four majors. Not coincidentally, it came just two short years after he started working with Dr. Jim Loehr, the Orlando sports psychologist who helped Dan Jansen so much.

"You have to invest in your mind," he says. "It's a muscle, and it does need to be trained. You don't just *become* mentally strong. It doesn't just *happen*."

The pair have created an effective and unusual strategy for positive visualization. Rose sometimes creates stories he'll tell himself on the golf course. He'll pretend he's playing an event where he had a good result, like the time in 2007 when he shot 65 in the Bob Hope Chrysler Classic and almost won the tournament. Whatever the story, the cardinal rule is that it has to avoid anything negative.

"It sometimes hurts more than the positive feels good," he says. "I think statistically you need eleven positive inputs to negate one negative. So that just shows you how really fragile we are mentally, and how you need to protect yourself. You need to protect yourself *from* yourself, really."

At just twenty-seven, and without any formal education beyond the age of sixteen, Justin Rose seems wise beyond his years and unusually intelligent and mature. But that didn't start at breakfast this morning. Hopkins remembers a decade earlier during that horrid stretch of missed cuts, when he and other journalists would wait each week outside the scorers' tent.

"Justin's father said to him at one stage, 'Look, you don't need to do this; you don't need to see these guys. You can go out the back door and I can spirit you away. You don't need to go through the anguish of having to explain to them yet again why you failed.' And he said, 'No,

I need to do this. I need to learn how to do this. It will stand me in good stead.' And you and I both know there are plenty of players we could name who would have done that once or twice and then headed out the back entrance and avoided the journalists."

As we sit in the dining room in Orlando that June morning, it's clear that Rose has thought long, hard, and without bitterness—although it's hard to understand how—about a career that has meandered to every point on the emotional compass.

"What I went through as a young pro made me the competitor I am today."

Chapter 7

GREG NORMAN

*"Show me a path with no obstacles and
that path will lead you nowhere."*

Sometimes it's easy to see the perverse humor in a slump—unless, of course, it's *your* slump. Then it's not a slump. It's a conspiracy.

"It feels like everything's uphill against the wind," says PGA Tour veteran John Cook. "It feels like everything's lipping out and you're getting nothing but a bad draw every week. You feel like you can't hit the ball on the club face and the hole looks smaller than the ball."

In 1995, Cook was in the midst of a slump so cruel and unrelenting it eventually required something of an "intervention" from his fellow pros.

"They just cornered me and said: 'C'mon, man, you're not done yet.'"

That year, during the second round of the Memorial Tournament in Columbus, Ohio—the same town where Cook had been a college star at Ohio State—he hit his third shot at the par-five fifth hole with a little too much spin, and it sucked back off the green. Because of the wet conditions, lift, clean, and place rules were in effect. Angry at the world, Cook stormed up to pluck his ball off the turf, but when he swiped at it, he mistakenly swatted the ball into a nearby creek. Oops. A moment earlier he was thinking that the wedge he'd hit was going to be close enough to give him a good look at a birdie. Minutes later, he had carded a triple bogey.

"And I said, 'OK, here we go, now you've hit the absolute bottom of the barrel.' I was so mad, I actually started to laugh, and I thought: maybe this is the bottom. And you know what? Things actually started to get better soon after."

Slumps elicit anger and humor, and also the game's very own proprietary brand of self-pity. "Slump shame" is that particularly pathetic form of self-loathing that makes a man or a woman want to shrink back from playing with all but their closest companions—those who've seen it all and in front of whom they're simply incapable of feeling embarrassment.

So volcanic was my disgust with the state of *my* game that I actually once turned down an invitation to Pine Valley. I thought it couldn't possibly get any more extreme than that, but then the phone rang.

"Hi, this is Trina from Greg Norman's office," the pleasant voice on the other end of the line said. "Greg wants to know if you're available to play golf with him on March 5."

Oh no.

In late December 2007, Norman had agreed to talk with me for this book. He said he'd have his office call to try and set up a time that worked for both of us. This wasn't quite what I had in mind. I quickly sent him an e-mail: "Greg, I'm trying to find my way out of an embarrassing slump, I haven't picked up a club in five months, I have a bad back, and you want to play golf with me? You think this is a good idea?"

There's really no graceful way out. We meet at Emerald Dunes Country Club in West Palm Beach, Florida. Tim Rosaforte, senior writer for *Golf World* magazine, and Norman's friend Jay Margolis, who sits on the board of the McGregor Golf Equipment Company—of which Norman is president—join us. We decide to play Norman against the best ball of our three. No strokes. I am far from optimistic, but on the range I hit the ball decently as we warm up.

"What's all this nonsense about a slump?" Norman bellows from behind me.

I wonder how many pro-am rounds he had to suffer over the years with chops like me and how many times this man who was once golf's greatest attraction had bolstered an amateur's confidence with gracious—and patently false—praise.

"What do you think?" I ask him. "Are slumps like heart attacks, or are they like headaches?" I'm trying to figure out if this man who's had so much adversity in his golfing life thinks that slumps are fatal or just bothersome.

"Oh, I'd definitely say headaches," he answers without missing a beat, "because headaches come from either stress, aggravation, frustration, or whatever it is, and you can get rid of a headache by calming things out. And it's the same thing with a slump."

We adjourn to the first hole, a 501-yard par five with bunkers and water down the right. I eventually miss a twenty-footer for par, after the Shark burns the edge with his birdie try. I'm not hyperventilating, but I'm clearly having trouble "calming things out" playing alongside a guy whose irons are all worn—exactly at the sweet spot—with a perfectly round mark precisely the size of a golf ball.

We've played one hole, and my head is filled with a million things, none of which have anything to do with just enjoying myself.

"You know, we're all our own worst enemies," says Norman, "and we won't admit it." The man speaks from experience.

In 1991 Norman was obliviously plodding along, vaguely aware that something was wrong but not sure exactly what it was. With ten PGA Tour wins, and another forty-eight around the world, including the 1986 British Open, he had become the game's biggest star. Four times, starting in 1986, he'd ended a season as the world's top-ranked player, but now he'd gone two years without a win anywhere. It was the first slump of his career, and he was getting pummeled by the enemy within.

"I was driving to Old Marsh," he says of the high-end Palm Beach Gardens club where the Shark played his golf at the time, "and I was in a convertible, and for some reason I just pulled over to the side of the road, and I stopped and I put the seat back on the driver's side and I just laid there staring at the clouds.

"And I said to myself, 'What the fuck am I going to the course for?' I said, 'What are your intentions? What do you want to do? Do you want to get better? Do you want to get out of this thing? What's your attitude?'"

Norman says he sat there for perhaps forty minutes just staring at the clouds and talking to himself. "I swear I could take you to that spot today. It was on Hood Road."

Then he put the seat up, continued on to Old Marsh, and, for the first time in a long time, practiced with "a free mind." It was an epiphany.

"If you go to the golf course with a lot of baggage in your head," he says, "you won't be able to go there with the approach to do the job you need to do. I used that moment with the roof off, looking at the clouds, quite a few times in my career."

Norman also had another mental trick. He would put his head down so that his wide-brimmed straw hat obscured any view of his face, and while cloistered in his own private world he would jam his thumb into his stomach just below his rib cage with such force that the pain would bring tears. It was his way of bringing—demanding—focus.

Eventually, with the help of Butch Harmon, Norman was able to relocate the form that had initially catapulted him to fame. Harmon is one of the game's most astute technicians, but his contribution started off having little to do with technique. In Houston for the completion of an event that had been postponed from earlier in the year, Norman asked if Harmon would watch while he hit a few balls on the range.

"He handed me a two-iron," remembers Norman, "and said, 'I'm going to get you back to hitting it high and hitting it left and hitting it right like you used to, and I'm going to get your confidence back.' And I thought, 'Wow, nobody's ever said that before!' He wanted to work on my confidence."

"There were a few things in his swing we worked on," says Harmon, "but it was mostly about getting him back to being Greg Norman."

In September 1992, Norman broke a thirty-month slump and won the Canadian Open. His career included nine more PGA Tour wins, including a second British Open, and in one of the great weeks ever at the Tour's premier event, he won the 1994 Players Championship by shooting 24 under par—a record that may never be broken.

But as much as Norman's life is defined by what he did, it is equally framed by what he failed to accomplish. He says his biggest disappointment was coming away from the 1986 season with only a single major title—the British Open—when he'd led all four that year going into the final round.

"I look back and think of just one or two shots that I'd played differently in each tournament and I could have won," he says. "I'll tell you what: I don't think there's any doubt in my mind a guy could win the [calendar] grand slam." Which "guy" is left unsaid, but it's not as if there's any ambiguity about who he had in mind.

Norman never made it any secret that the Masters was the tournament he most wanted to win, maybe because it's where he first became famous. In his first trip to Augusta in 1981, he led the Masters after the opening round. At twenty-six, he was an exotic curiosity and became that year's "it" story. He finished fourth and came away with a nickname that stuck: the Great White Shark. But over the years, Augusta teased him. He finished in the top five on eight different occasions, and some of his near misses seemed cruel. In 1987, Larry Mize chipped in from forty-five yards to beat him in a playoff. A year earlier, Jack Nicklaus shot 30 on the back nine to win his sixth green jacket at the improbable age of forty-six. Norman responded to the Nicklaus charge by putting on one of his own. He birdied 14, 15, 16, and 17 to pull even with the Golden Bear, who had already finished, but then peeled a four-iron wide right of the green and bogeyed the eighteenth hole to miss forcing a playoff by a stroke.

"If I could have one shot in my life back," says Norman, "it would be that one."

All day long, Norman had been swinging aggressively and effectively, but standing in the middle of the eighteenth fairway, he altered his strategy. He chose a soft four-iron rather than a hard five. The shot, he says was poorly executed, but before that it was simply a bad decision.

"I was kinda crushed after '86," he says.

To many, though, the more shocking and gruesomely memorable "almost" in Norman's career came a decade later. He opened that year by tying the course record with 63, and by Saturday night he stood at 13 under par with a six-stroke lead over Nick Faldo. But on Sunday morning, Norman woke up with a stiff back and, what was worse, a swing that was suddenly out of synch.

"No matter what I tried to do in a short period of time [on the range]," he says, "I couldn't get the club squared up."

Because his swing wasn't working, Norman says his confidence fared even worse. It turned into a disastrous snowball, which over the next four-plus hours did nothing but gather momentum. Coming off the eighth green, the lead had been halved to three. By the twelfth tee box, it was gone entirely, and when Norman stepped up and deposited his tee shot there into Rae's Creek, for the first time all week he wasn't the leader. Faldo went on to win by five. But what turned out to be perhaps the greatest professional failure of Norman's life became at the same time one of his biggest personal triumphs.

Dazed after having just blown the largest final-round lead in major golf championship history, Norman was sitting in the scorers' tent directly after the round when something popped into his head. He thought of two players (whom he wouldn't name) who had somehow lost major championships but had then skulked away without talking to the press.

"And I thought to myself, you know what? I ain't going to be that guy," he says. "I've got to suck it up. I'm going to take my medicine. The best thing I did was go straight into the press conference."

What followed was a forty-five-minute confessional. Norman bared his soul.

"I screwed up," he told the assembled media, many of whom were accustomed to far less candor from, and access to, those who had lost so ingloriously. "It's all on me. I know that, but losing the Masters is not the end of the world. I let this one get away, but I still have a pretty good life. I'll wake up tomorrow still breathing, I hope. All these hiccups I have, they must be for a reason. All this is just a test. I just don't know what the test is yet."

Instantly, everything changed. The man who only hours before had been the object of ridicule was now the object of admiration.

"The way he handled himself was amazing," says Nick Faldo. "I don't know if I would have been strong enough."

"That was his finest moment," says Davis Love III.

Norman got thousands of letters of support (a Sydney newspaper had given out his fax number). The following week when he showed up to play at Hilton Head, instead of withdrawing as many expected him to do, he was the star of the tournament, overshadowing even the Masters champion, Nick Faldo, who was also in the field.

"He said, in a way, this was the best thing that ever happened to him," recalls CBS's Jim Nantz, who had dinner with Norman on his boat that week, "because he got to find out how much people really cared about him."

Love saw Norman playing the ninth hole during a practice round and actually walked out to meet him and escort him in.

"You were just two swings away," Love says he told him. "If you'd just gotten it on the green on seven and nine, you'd have run away with the tournament. I said you're going to win plenty of them as soon as you get one, or something like that."

"It was just so encouraging," says Norman.

Soon afterward, Norman had shoulder and hip surgery to correct problems that might have contributed to his poor Sunday showing at Augusta. And despite the prevailing opinion that the loss would finish him, he went on to win twice more on the PGA Tour.

"I've learned how to deal with things on such a tough level in a lot of ways," says the man whom Paul Azinger called "golf's greatest victim."

"I'm a very resilient person."

Back at Emerald Dunes now, I am having an extraordinarily mediocre day. I turn in 45. The Shark is even. He effortlessly launches a three-metal into the tenth fairway and then poses with that iconic look I've seen a thousand times: searing blue eyes hopefully trying to guide the ball's flight as he bites the inside of his cheek. He was the world's number one player for a then-record 331 weeks. In 2001, he was inducted into the World Golf Hall of Fame with the highest percentage of votes of anyone ever elected. Worldwide, he's won eighty-six tournaments, and it's not an uncommon opinion that he might have been the greatest driver of the golf ball ever. Yet, despite it all, he knows that might not be his legacy. Norman says there is nothing he can do about that but put it to good use.

"I always address my career not on my successes, but on my failures," he says. "I've got this little thing written on my desk, and I can't remember who the quote came from, but it says, 'Show me a path with no obstacles, and that path will lead you nowhere.'"

This is classic Norman, who has always been Don Quixote—occasionally tilting at windmills—on an endless trek to find answers, and not just about golf.

"If I had a different thought than somebody else," he says, "I always wanted to know why I was right or wrong."

But for all the searching Norman has done, from Zen books and Tony Robbins to maniacal physical preparedness, it's ironic that only *after* the conclusion of his competitive career did he find the counsel he found most lucid and valuable. "She would have helped me definitely," he says.

We are talking about his soon-to-be wife, Chris Evert, the eighteen-time major championship–winning tennis Hall of Famer.

"It's the first time in our lives that we can actually sit down and feel like somebody can relate to where we've been and what we've had to go through. Our conversations have been very powerful in a lot of ways. I'm not going to talk about any of the things she's told me, because they're things she's never mentioned to anybody else before—about some of her matches with Martina."

I nod respectfully, and the next night I call Evert, who is an old friend and colleague. She talks about her struggles against Navratilova, to whom she once lost thirteen consecutive times, and Tracy Austin, who beat Evert five straight.

"I had to figure a way out of that," she remembers.

Evert says that in tennis, as in golf, she believes that a slump is primarily about two things: fundamentals and confidence.

"I went on the court with her [Navratilova] thirteen times in a row knowing I was going to lose, so I lost. Then the fourteenth time, the first thing I did was to get back to basics, which for me was my ground stroke game. Then in a certain sense, I puffed out my chest and kind of bluffed myself and said, 'I'm going to win this match.' I didn't fully believe it, but I still went through the body language of 'Chrissie, just show her, and show yourself some confidence!' I almost played games with my mind: 'C'mon, you're going to do it, you're going to do it,' even though deep down I was confused, like, 'I think I can do it, but I might not.'"

The same thing happened with Austin. In the 1980 U.S. Open semifinals, Evert dropped the first set, but then she rallied and never lost to Austin again. "Whoever it was that said 'protect your confidence at all costs' [David Duval], that was just brilliant," she says.

It was tending to his own diminished confidence that lifted Norman out of his first slump years before, but he thinks that for the average golfer the bigger issue might be realistic expectations. Too many people, he thinks, have a clouded view of their capabilities. They play from tees they shouldn't and are angry and confused when they don't execute perfectly every time they pull a club. Norman is happy when he hits four perfect shots a round. "We're never going to hit the ball dead solid flush perfect every time."

"So you think people have unrealistic expectations?" I ask.

"Definitely."

We're sitting in the grill room now. Norman's afternoon consists of business (during the round he talked about golf course design projects in India and Dubai) and what has now become a staple of his day: tennis.

"Chrissie says my athletic talent was wasted on golf," he laughs.

On this day, the Shark swallowed the three guppies who tried to take him on. He shot four under and closed us out on the fifteenth hole. I shot 90. Today he wins easily, but golf isn't always like that. Neither is life. No one knows that better than Norman. The man speaks from experience.

Chapter 8

PHIL MICKELSON

*"I think you find people who—the trials in their lives
can become their identities. They take it on and it becomes them.
We don't live our lives that way"*

I am sitting in a Miami hotel room with Phil Mickelson, and we are fencing. It might appear as if we are simply talking and watching a basketball game on television, but that is not the case.

We are fencing.

I ask a question; he answers, sometimes barely, always cautiously.

"Did you have a time that was terribly difficult for you in golf?"

"No," he says.

No?

So it goes. Thrust and parry.

"What about 2003?" I ask, referring to his worst year ever as a professional on Tour, when he dropped from second on the money list to thirty-eighth.

"It was frustrating," he says, and then offers nothing more.

Frustrating? That's it? One top-three finish, and nothing better, after having won eight times the preceding three years? Nothing more than simply *frustrating*?

It's as if Mickelson is playing a straight-away and reachable par five, and choosing to lay up. The oddity, of course, is that Phil Mickelson is not the type of person who lays up very often. That aggressive Arnold Palmer–like quality once led to a Ford advertising campaign constructed entirely around the slogan "What will Phil do next?"

But it wasn't only what he *did*. Intelligent and opinionated, Mickelson has been known to more than occasionally pull the *verbal* big stick out of his bag and let loose. There was the time in 2003 when he criticized Tiger Woods's equipment, saying in *Golf* magazine, "He hates that I can fly it past him now. He has a faster swing speed than I do, but he has inferior equipment. Tiger is the only player who is good enough to overcome the equipment he's stuck with."

A year before, Mickelson was fighting for the lead in the final round of the Bay Hill Invitational when he bogeyed the then par-five sixteenth hole with a questionably aggressive play. After the round, he told my NBC colleague Mark Rolfing that he didn't care what people said. This was how he played, and he wasn't changing his game.

As children we're all told that honesty is the best policy. It hasn't always worked out that way for Mickelson. A media establishment, starved for something beyond the bland and empty pabulum it is frequently fed, listened eagerly to his comments and then in many cases, turned around to roast him for his candor and color. You can see how it's a no-win situation. So I try again, through a different door.

"Did you know what was going on?" I ask him.

"If I knew what was wrong, I would have fixed it," he says.

In 2003, Mickelson was furiously pedaling a bicycle on which the chain wasn't attached to the wheel.

"I was working on things, but they were never the right things. I was putting in time, but I was just moving laterally. I wasn't moving towards an endpoint. I wasn't getting better."

The reality is, he was actually getting worse. Mickelson hit 18 percent fewer fairways than he did the year before and dropped sixty-one places in the greens-in-regulation ranking. He went from having the third best final round scoring average on Tour to one that was ranked 147th. Oddly, his best finish all year came at a venue that normally exposes and magnifies inexact play. He placed third at the Masters, but he did so almost totally on the basis of a sparkling short game. Very little else was working.

On the range that week, his long-time caddy, Jim "Bones" McKay, remembers watching Mickelson trying to hit shots at a flag that was 210 yards away, and missing perhaps eight in ten attempts by fifty feet.

"It got to the point that week," says McKay, "and it's kind of representative of the whole year, that he couldn't fix what he was doing, so he would sit in the room where he was staying and *imagine* himself hitting good shots because he couldn't [actually] hit good shots."

An accounting of his next nine tournaments reads like that of a struggling journeyman rather than a man who started the season ranked number two in the world. Outside a missed cut in Washington, Mickelson averaged finishing in 44th position, and he never placed higher than 13th. What not many people knew at the time was that he was battling to stay upright through an enormous emotional and psychological squall.

"I think," says Rick Smith, his teacher at the time, "it was one of those high-impact moments where you start to really wonder what your purpose is . . . how fragile life is and how easily it could have been taken away. "

On March 23, Amy Mickelson gave birth to the couple's third child. It had been a difficult pregnancy—Amy had been on bed rest since November and had been in and out of the hospital because of almost constant preterm labor—but Evan Mickelson's arrival was beyond difficult. It was terrifying.

Early that day, the Mickelsons headed off to Scripps La Jolla Hospital, where Amy, who was past due, was going to be induced.

"I'd been in labor for five months," she says, "and the doctor said, 'This is going to take literally fifteen minutes and you're going to have your baby. I just don't see how this is going to be difficult.' "

What her obstetrician didn't know was that a large piece of scar tissue had formed in the birth canal, which was holding Evan in, so the delivery that was supposed to take fifteen minutes went on all day and into the night. Ironically, the very same mass that was now creating the problem had probably saved Evan's life; during all that preterm labor, it was the only thing that had kept him in the womb and allowed him to develop normally. When the child finally pushed through the obstruction, he tore a six-inch hole in his mother's uterus. Amy Mickelson began to hemorrhage profusely and went into shock, while her son was fighting for his life, too.

"He didn't breathe for seven minutes," says Phil, "and there was a possibility of long-term brain damage."

Moments later, McKay and his wife arrived at the hospital.

"And here comes Phil," says the man who'd carried his bag and traveled the world by his side for ten years, "and I swear to you, he had no idea who I was. No idea. He looked at me like I was from Mars when I said hello to him."

Only two doctors in the country knew how to perform the complicated surgery that was now necessary to save Amy Mickelson's life. As luck would have it, one of them was in La Jolla that night, at dinner with his wife, just a few minutes from the hospital.

Much of that day is a blurry memory to Amy Mickelson, but there are small pieces she'll never forget. "I could hear Phil yelling 'Breathe, Evan, breathe!' I remember watching him during the surgery. They let him watch through this tiny little hole in the wall. It must have been very difficult to have his child in one room and me in the other and not know what the outcome was going to be for either of us."

Amy Mickelson stops talking. Her eyes begin to well up, and her voice becomes unsteady. It is Mother's Day as we sit talking in Ponte Vedra Beach, Florida, and she is retelling the only story about one of her children that maybe she would like to forget.

"I'm sorry," she says. "I never talk about this. We try not to live in the past."

Both Amy and Evan recovered, but Mickelson's golf game, at least in the short term, did not.

"I was kind of numb for a while," he says. "I didn't care [about golf]. I was more worried about her [Amy's] health. I was more worried about my son's health. I think that probably throughout the year I didn't put the same mental energy into my game."

At the end of November, Mickelson put his tortured season to bed and then went to work. He called Smith and Dave Pelz and asked the two instructors to come up with a game plan.

"What do I have to do to win majors?" Smith says Mickelson asked him. "I need to start winning some of these bigger events, and not just winning in the desert and out in California."

Two primary areas were identified. The first was driving accuracy, where in 2003, Mickelson was among the worst on Tour. "I tried to eliminate a hook and only hit slices," he says. "I tried to eliminate the right side of the golf course."

It was the same strategy Jack Nicklaus had used a generation before, not to lift himself out of a slump, but as an everyday game plan. A hook—a left-to-right curving shot for a lefty—can be difficult to control. But a fade—the opposite shot—generally tends to stay more in the neighborhood where it is hit. In a January visit to southern California, Smith and Mickelson worked from sunup to sunset on quieting a lower body that had become overactive and caused the problem. In four days, Mickelson went from drawing the ball to fading it.

"So I could aim down the right side and take that out of play and not worry about it," says Mickelson. "I tried to simplify my game."

Mickelson's other chief off-season concern was to maximize his scoring opportunities.

"Phil wanted to become much more efficient inside of 150 yards," says McKay, "because he realized that one of the ways you get it done out here is to make birdies when you're hitting wedges and nine-irons."

So Mickelson and Pelz worked hard and quietly in December 2003 to develop an alternate type of shot suited just for those opportunities. Called, appropriately enough, a "Pelz," it employs a shorter backswing and a flatter flight, and it doesn't impart as much spin. "It's about ten to twelve yards off my full yardage on a club," he says. Mickelson could use it 85 percent of the time, only going to the more conventional swing when the greens were extremely firm, or the pins were tucked in relatively inaccessible locations. He practiced by placing towels at various distances and trying to hit them.

In the third week of January 2004, he emerged from his competitive hibernation at the Bob Hope Chrysler Classic. As is his routine, Mickelson grabbed McKay and headed off to another course near the tournament venue to practice in private.

"So here we are at the back of the range at this golf course in Palm Springs," says McKay, "and he says, this is what I'm doing now, and I'm scrambling. I'm trying to figure out where the towels go and whatever else. And I'm like, 'Holy shit, did you write me a letter and it just didn't show up?' I didn't have a clue."

If McKay was surprised, he wasn't alone. The golf establishment was shocked as Mickelson looked nothing like the player it had last seen. He shot 30 under par that week and beat Skip Kendal in a playoff. "It's too soon to tell," wrote Ken Fidlin presciently in the *Toronto Sun,* "but this could be Phil Mickelson's year."

But it wasn't only the win, his first in eighteen months; it was how he did it. Mickelson hit the fairway more than

72 percent of the time. His season average the year before was just under 49 percent. And he was just getting started. In his first eleven events of 2004, Mickelson finished in the top five or better eight times. Only once was he out of the top ten. Now that he had identified what was wrong in the off season, the first domino had fallen.

"The most frustrating thing," he says, "is not knowing what needs to be done, because it feels like every time you practice, it's just a waste of time. When I saw improvement in my practice sessions, I was much more confident on the golf course, and there was a carryover effect."

The best was yet to come. At Augusta, Mickelson birdied five of the last seven holes, held off a furious charge from Ernie Els, and finally won his elusive first major. Both his "Pelz" shot and the new driving strategy were crucial elements of the win.

"When I stood up on tee boxes, I just knew the ball was going to go in the middle of the fairway," he told a packed press room after the win. "The hours that I spent with Dave Pelz, getting the yardages down with the wedges, those hours of work and having that proper direction, I ultimately knew or did not ever lack belief that I would ultimately win."

For years, Mickelson had trudged to one media center after another at major championships only to answer a tired but legitimate question: Why hadn't he won one of these things yet? The answer was always the same: "I thought by now I would have won several."

Sitting in the Miami hotel room, with the basketball game now just so much background noise, I ask Mickelson if that April day in Georgia when the monkey fell off his back was the most important day in his golf career.

He surprises me.

"I think it was the second," he says. "The Tucson Open was the first."

In 1991, as a college junior, at the tender age of twenty, Phil Mickelson became only the fourth amateur to win a PGA Tour event since World War II. No one has done it since. It was the capstone on a nearly incomparable amateur career that had started in the backyard of his San Diego home, with his father demonstrating the golf swing right-handed, and the son—a natural righty—assuming a left-handed stance so he could face his dad and more easily mirror his movements. On his way up the ladder, Mickelson would win the 1990 U.S. Amateur and the NCAA individual title a record-tying three times. While outrageous, the win in Tucson, given his trajectory, somehow didn't seem inconceivable, and for Mickelson it meant more than just another trophy (one of the most distinctive and—truth be told—goofiest in Tour history: the "Conquistador's helmet").

"It gave me a chance to graduate from college," he says, "and come out on Tour on *my* time schedule with fully exempt status. It gave me opportunities off the golf course that were significant and allowed me to be comfortable and set for the rest of my life."

The Masters win thirteen years later was different. It was pure emotion, and it was enormously popular. For all his prodigious talent, over the years there had become something about him with which so many people could identify. In a way, he was Sisyphus, and he had finally nudged the rock over the peak of the hill.

"I remember sitting down that night in the Augusta clubhouse," says Smith, "and he said, 'Let's go get the next one. Let's go get them all.'"

And he almost did. Two months later at Shinnecock, it took one of the great final-round putting performances of all time for Retief Goosen to win the U.S. Open. The title wasn't decided until the next-to-last hole where Mickelson put his tee shot in the bunker and then three-putted for double bogey. A month later, he finished one shot out of a playoff at the British Open, and then in August, two shots out of a playoff at the PGA. It was a spectacular year with two wins and thirteen top tens. At the majors he finished first, second, third, and sixth. Mickelson had smoothly and impressively navigated his way out of the worst slump of his career. Little did he realize amidst the delirium and near perfection of 2004 that the rudiments that had rescued him from the confusion and malaise of a year before would sow the seeds for one of the worst weeks of his golf life.

In June 2006, a new and once thought to be inconceivable world order seemed to be taking shape. Since the turn of the century, the question had been repeatedly asked: Who would step up to challenge the supremacy of Tiger Woods? On the heels of his impressive 2004, the answer now appeared to be Phil Mickelson. In August 2005, he won the PGA at Baltusrol, his second major championship. Eight months later, he made it two straight when he won the Masters. As the U.S. Open arrived at Winged Foot, just outside New York, Mickelson had as many wins for the season (two) as did Woods, who was returning to competition after a two-month layoff following the death of his father.

"Can't wait for Thursday to start," a relaxed Mickelson told the assembled media on Tuesday that week. "Looking forward to it."

When Woods missed the cut—his first as a professional at a major championship—the door was wide open. Mickelson's one under par 69 in the third round vaulted him into a tie for the lead. But as he went to sleep Saturday night on the brink of a third straight major championship, he knew his position was precarious.

"I had played some of the best golf of my life in the Masters that year," he says, "and the week before [the Masters] I won in Atlanta by thirteen shots. I was playing phenomenal. But I wasn't able to get that performance level back."

The very tonic that had revitalized his game—a fade—had suddenly developed an exaggerated character and was now a full-blown slice. Only weeks before, driving had been one of the strengths of Mickelson's game. Now, at the worst possible time, it had turned into a glaring weakness. On almost half the par-fours and par-fives during the first three days of the championship, his tee shot wound up in the rough.

"I was trying not to think about it," he says. "I knew I wasn't hitting very many fairways. I knew I was struggling with that, but I kept trying to fix it on the range, and we just couldn't get it done."

Mickelson's driving was so out of sorts, says McKay, that "he was teeing up golf balls on the edge of the putting green and driving them over the putting green into the range three minutes before our tee time. He just didn't have it."

Like a rowboat bobbing up and down in rough seas, Mickelson fought all day Sunday to keep himself upright. He hit just two fairways. In one of the cruelest and most ironic twists of the week, his drive on the seventeenth hole landed in a garbage receptacle. He had literally driven it in to the junk. Still, he made par, and he stood on the seventy-second hole of his nation's championship needing only a par to win the title outright or a bogey to make it into a playoff.

But on the final hole, he hit a wild slice, which bounced off a hospitality tent and came to rest behind a grove of trees. It was hardly what Mickelson had in mind, but given the way he had driven the ball all week, not an enormous surprise—and, despite the drama, far from the end of the championship. "The drive didn't end up costing him the tournament," says Smith. "It was the second shot."

Mickelson tried to cut a three-iron around the trees but failed to get the "around" part to work and squarely hit one of the Norwegian maples he was trying to circum-navigate. The ball rolled back not far from its original position. "It was the worst shot he hit all week," said one close observer.

From there he hit another three-iron into a greenside bunker and failed to get up and down. Phil Mickelson's double bogey six at the last hole had lost him the title he craved above all others in the game. "I'm such an idiot," he famously said in the aftermath.

"It's one of the toughest things I've ever gone through," he says as we sit—no longer fencing—in his Miami hotel room. "To be so close on the last hole, after driving it ter-ribly all week—not just the last day, but all week, driving it terribly, and getting up and down from everywhere and fighting to stay in the tournament and then to give it away was disappointing."

The popular perception was that Mickelson was ruined, that he might never get beyond the Winged Foot disaster, but there he was three days later at Disney World with friends and family, smiling as if nothing had hap-pened. And everyone you talk to in the Mickelson camp says pretty much the same thing. He really *was* able to turn the page.

"We're not the kind of people who hold on to our stuff," Amy Mickelson says, reiterating a theme we had talked about earlier. "I think you find people who, their trials in their lives can become their identities. They take it on, and it becomes them. We don't live our lives that way."

"So how do you think you deal with adversity?" I ask her husband. "You think you're good at it?"

"I've kind of had to be," laughs the man who had so many celebrated heartbreaks before he won his first major in his forty-seventh try. "I've had a lot of adversity in my career."

Ten months after Winged Foot, Mickelson parted ways with Smith and started working with Butch Harmon. Despite the fact that he'd won at Pebble Beach early in the 2007 season, Mickelson was still thinking about what had happened at the Open.

"Sometimes you need a catalyst to get you better," he says. "I was so close to winning that event, but had I won, I wouldn't have taken the steps to get where I am now."

In his first week working with Harmon, Mickelson won the prestigious Players by shortening his notoriously long swing, altering his footwork, and thus regaining accuracy and confidence. The mechanics seemed to click right away.

"The big problem with Phil was on his sight lines," says

Harmon, "because he was so used to hitting big curves. Before, he couldn't hit the little subtle ones."

Now, almost instantly, he could. But despite all the technical adjustments, Mickelson, like many players, believes that to play good golf you have to feel good *about* your golf, so he developed a drill to work on his confidence.

"I believe you start at the hole and work out," he says. "I don't believe you start practice or preparation from the tee and work in. I think the majority of the game revolves around the hole."

Mickelson finds a spot where he feels bulletproof, say three feet. To reinforce the feeling, he putts a hundred balls from that distance. But feeling confident from three feet actually gives you a six-foot circle in which to land the ball (three feet on either side of the cup). Now, if you've missed the green or need to lag a putt, you have a six-foot comfort zone as a target.

"I believe most people's struggles with their golf games have to do with their short games," he says. "You've got to see the ball go in the hole, and it just builds confidence. As soon as I start making it from three feet, I'll start trying to get six footers, then 15 footers."

And in keeping with this theory that you need to spend more time around the hole, whenever Mickelson feels the rhythm on his driving go awry, he immediately heads to a greenside bunker.

"You wouldn't think there'd be a correlation, but when

you hit a bunker shot, there's no 'hit.' You have to swing the club and let the club do the work through the sand. You have to swing it fluid. You can't try to power it, or give it a little extra hit at impact, because you won't hit it well. So you keep this rhythm . . . this rhythmic swing from the bunker. It carries over to your driving."

This is pure Mickelson: always looking for an answer. Curious and thoughtful, he seems to have lived a life looking for answers, even when a question doesn't appear to have been asked. Like a racehorse champing at the bit, he wants to run, to go for broke. You get the impression that he will fight that instinct for as long as he lives, partially because he always thinks he can pull it off, no matter what "it" is.

"He goes on his own path," says Amy Mickelson, "whether it's right or wrong. I love that about him, because he's not going to go with the grain. Right or wrong, he's an independent thinker."

There is no doubt Phil Mickelson is a decisive and strong-willed man. We spent an hour or so together talking in a Miami hotel room, as well as several other encounters on driving ranges, around putting greens, and in locker rooms throughout the Tour season. Still, I can't help thinking: when there are no microphones or cameras or notepads around, how much fencing does he do with himself?

Chapter 9

BEN CRENSHAW

"As for the swing, it has to be yours."

In golf, a bad memory—or no memory at all—can be very handy, if not essential. "Throw up on yourself," as they say on Tour when describing a horrible day, and a touch of amnesia is probably a good thing. But it also works the other way. Let's say you're Ben Crenshaw. You'd want to do everything you possibly could to remember, because there was a time when Crenshaw was impossibly good. As an amateur and novice professional, he was a cartoonish amalgam of not only charisma and modesty but good looks and better talent.

"He was just a superstar," says Roger Maltbie. "He was the one you heard about. He could hit it a mile, and he could putt better than anybody else."

At the age of ten he shot 74 for eighteen holes. By age thirteen he'd qualified for the prestigious Texas State Junior; by sixteen he'd won it twice. As a high school senior, a time when many of his classmates might have been reading about world-class sports competition, Crenshaw was knee-deep in the middle of it. He qualified for the 1970 U.S. Open at Hazeltine National outside Minneapolis. The week's early highlight was a trip to Metropolitan Stadium with his father and seeing the Twins' Harmon Killebrew hit a massive home run. But once the Open started, Crenshaw wasn't so much watching sports highlights as making them. On a cold and windy day, he shot 75 in the first round, just four strokes off the lead, and tied for eighth—and found himself summoned to the press room for the first time in his life. The customary procedure is for those who've played well to come and give the details of their birdies and bogeys, but when the United States Golf Association media official asked Crenshaw to go over his scorecard, the eighteen-year-old golfing ingénue responded literally: "Four, four, three . . ."

Laughing now at his naiveté, Crenshaw recalls the great golf writer Dan Jenkins noting, "This kid is greener than the fairways." But he sure could play. Crenshaw not only finished the championship tied for low amateur but beat Gary Player (tied for 44th), Jack Nicklaus (t-51st), and Arnold Palmer (t-54th). He'd played a practice round early in the week with Lee Trevino, who would later say that Crenshaw was "the best eighteen-year-old golfer I've ever seen."

The rest of the year wasn't bad, either. Crenshaw played nineteen tournaments and won eighteen of them. The next few years was a blur of uninterrupted, and in some cases unprecedented, success as his career seemed to move at breakneck speed. He became the first freshman in history to win the NCAA individual title, and then went on to win it the next two years as well (the second was shared with his University of Texas friend and teammate Tom Kite). He won a staggering eighteen college tournaments during his three years at U-T. In the eleven PGA Tour events he played as an amateur, he never missed a single cut—a claim that neither Nicklaus nor Woods would be able to make. Back at the Open again in 1971 at Merion outside Philadelphia, he finished tied for 27th and got to meet his idol.

"I saw him go upstairs to the bathrooms by himself, and I said, 'Here's my chance.' So I go up there and follow him in and stick out my hand and say 'Jack, I'm Ben Crenshaw from Austin.'"

Jack Nicklaus was standing at the urinal, with his hands otherwise occupied.

"I was so nervous," says Crenshaw, "and Jack said, 'Wait a minute Ben, let me finish up here.'"

"He was so embarrassed," says Nicklaus, "but that's how we met, and we laugh about it now. 'Just a second, Ben, I'll be right with you.'"

When Crenshaw turned professional after his junior season in the summer of 1973, nothing seemed to change. He won the PGA Tour's qualifying tournament by a then-record twelve shots, and then he won the very first event in which he played as a Tour member. At that point in his life, Crenshaw knew exactly what a slump was: something that happened to someone else.

"Playing then was easy," says Crenshaw. "We were just playing."

"And not thinking too much about it," I say.

"I guess."

We are sitting in the grill room of the Broken Sound Golf Club in Boca Raton, Florida. Crenshaw is tied for 7th going into the final round of the Champions Tour's Allianz Championship after a pair of 68s. Now age fifty-six, the World Golf Hall of Fame member hasn't won an individual tournament of any kind in thirteen years—a fact with which he's not happy, but not preoccupied either. *Golf Digest* magazine once proclaimed that he's had more comebacks than John Travolta.

"I was gone twenty times. I'm not kidding you. Just lost, no confidence at all," says Crenshaw of his frequent slumps. "You just have to claw your way back. It happens to most of us."

Crenshaw's first slump hit him like an avalanche. He was twenty-two and had already won on Tour a handful of times. All of a sudden, it wasn't so easy. What he didn't realize at the time was that it wasn't the end of the world; it was just how the world actually works . . . in golf.

"Some people can't putt or they can't hit a bunker shot," he says, "or in my case, I was extremely wild off the tee. I just couldn't keep the ball in the ballpark. It was subject to go anywhere. I mean, it's a helpless feeling.

"I don't know if my experiences are too much different than anybody else's, because it's a difficult game to play. You have real good years, and then you kind of backslide in different departments. You do well for a period of time, and then you suffer in *another* department. You're lost, and you need to start over. And usually what happens is that you stop relying on *your* instinct."

Golfers, professional or otherwise, are always searching for "the secret," which is not a problem, says Crenshaw, as long as they know where to look and where not to. He remembers reading that Sam Snead claimed to look away when he was playing with Ben Hogan. Snead didn't like to watch the Hawk hit because his swing was so much faster than his own. "That's a wonderful way to think on the golf course," he says. As for the swing, "It has to be *yours*."

Crenshaw often cites the wisdom of the Texas Apostles: men like Harvey Penick, Crenshaw's long-time teacher; Dave Marr, the witty television commentator who won the 1965 PGA Championship; and Jackie Burke, the two-time major champion and Hall of Famer.

"I remember one of the great things Jackie said to me when I was very young," Crenshaw recalls. "He said, 'Ben, what's going to happen out there on Tour is you're going to see a successful player. He might have won the week before. He'll go out on the practice tee and he'll have a little crowd around him, and players will be kind of looking over their shoulders at him. Looking and seeing how he's doing what he's doing, and they'll say: 'Maybe I need to do that.' Jackie said that's when you need to take your shag bag and go to the other end of the range.

"Dave Marr and Harvey and those people—they possessed a lot of wisdom, and each of them thought along the same line. You can't do things like other people. You've got to find your own mechanism."

(Not surprisingly, that's how Crenshaw and his business partner Bill Coore run their highly successful golf course design firm as well: very distinctive, individualistic work that has resulted in some of the most critically acclaimed layouts in the past decade or so, such as Sand Hills in Nebraska, and Friar's Head on the east end of New York's Long Island.)

But no one was more responsible for shepherding Crenshaw's career than the self-effacing and simple Penick. In 1992, he published a collection of lessons and observations on the game of golf. When his son Tinsley originally told him about the book's advance, Penick was concerned because he didn't know if he could raise the money. He didn't understand that the advance was money that would be paid to *him*. *Harvey Penick's Little Red Book* eventually became the best-selling sports book of all time. It was based on simplicity and common sense and was really nothing more than the things Penick had been telling Crenshaw since the promising golfer first showed up on his lesson tee at age six.

"Harvey taught all of us to know that a different position at the ball will make you swing differently," says Crenshaw. "A ball that's up in your stance will delay your hip. A ball that's back in your stance, you'll cover that ball quickly. It's very much how you set up. The fundamentals are right there in front of you, and when you're in a weakened state of mind, believe me, you'll try anything to get back."

That's about where Crenshaw was in April 1995, hardly playing his best golf and maybe just a little bit desperate. Entering the Masters, he'd missed the cut the preceding week in New Orleans. "I remember I played with him those first two rounds, and he was just really struggling," says Davis Love III. "He broke his putter and had to putt with a two-iron or something. It wasn't good."

On the Sunday before the start of the Masters, Penick, who had been gravely ill, died. Crenshaw went to Augusta, played two practice rounds, and then went to Austin to serve as a pallbearer for the funeral before returning to Georgia for the tournament. He'd missed the cut in three of the previous four tournaments, but all of a sudden, in a week of such overwhelming sadness, he started to hit the ball perfectly. His longtime Masters caddy, Carl Jackson, had made several observations about Crenshaw's swing, most importantly suggesting that he move the ball back in his stance. It was just the type of thing Penick might have said. "I swear," says Crenshaw, "it was as if he [Harvey] climbed into Carl's body. I have no idea how that happened."

If Crenshaw had been in a slump, by the time the tournament started he no longer was. In what turned out to be one of the most unlikely and magical weeks in the game's history, a grieving Crenshaw shot 14 under par and won his second Masters by one stroke over Love.

"To get around Augusta on four days with just five bogeys is hard to believe," he later said. "I can't explain it."

The period leading up to the 1995 Masters was hardly Crenshaw's worst slump, just his most dramatic Travolta-like reemergence. In 1985, things were much worse. He missed the cut in more than half the tournaments he played, failed to record a single top-ten finish, and fell all the way to 149th on the money list. It was a bleak year, with a pair of underlying causes.

"I didn't know that I had a thyroid problem," he says. "I was lost for three months. I mean, my short game went out the window." For that Crenshaw could take medication, but for the other primary issue scuttling his game, there was no effective treatment. He was going through a divorce.

"I think if you're having personal problems, it's hard to function," he says. "Sometimes when somebody has a really big slump, your personality's not on an even keel. Your life's turned upside down, and it's really debilitating."

The physical element of golf is one thing, but it might not be the most important thing.

"Bobby Jones said that the most difficult course is five inches long. That's the distance between your ears. I remember almost every slump I had, I felt like a basket case. It's not a good feeling. You're out in front of everybody, and they're looking at you implode. It's embarrassing."

But for all the times that Crenshaw has bobbed up out of a malaise, during the last and most triumphant time he never even touched a club. In the fall of 1999, the United States was in a terrible slump at the Ryder Cup. Team USA had won only two of the previous seven matches, and this time around, Crenshaw was the U.S. team captain at The Country Club just outside Boston. His firm belief that one of the biggest challenges in golf—sticking to your own script, no matter what's going on around you—is even more important at the Ryder Cup, and more difficult.

"It's the hardest thing to do as a participant," he says. "You're thinking of a million things other than your play, and you tell the players to play their own game. You say you've gotten here for a reason. Rely on your good instinct. And they look at you like you're crazy."

By Saturday night, the United States was on the verge of another loss to another European team it was supposed to beat. Going into the final-day singles matches, the Europeans had a 10–6 lead. No Ryder Cup team had ever made up a final-day deficit of more than two points, but Crenshaw ended his press conference Saturday evening by warning not to write his team off.

"I'm a big believer in fate," he famously said, "and I

have a good feeling about this. That's all I'm going to tell you."

The next day, the Americans went out and pulled off what has come to be known as the Miracle at Brookline, winning 8½ out of a possible 12 points and ending the Ryder Cup slump.

"It's all because of Ben Crenshaw," Love told CNN/SI. "He fired us up, made us believe we could do it."

The captain busted the slump by helping his team believe that the five-inch course they were facing wasn't quite as formidable as they might have thought.

The dining room has emptied out now. A savage thunderstorm that stopped play an hour and a half earlier has scattered players and their families back to their hotels or to early dinners, or to wherever they go to pass the huge chunks of idle time out on Tour. Crenshaw, though, remains. He is gracious and has made a commitment, so he stays. But there is something more. This, after all, is a man who owns five hundred golf books and has had cats named Francis (Ouimet), Bobby (Jones), and Ben (Hogan). You get the idea he would talk all day and night about the game's mysteries. It's clear his mantra is to try and refine what you have instead of doing things the way other people do. But I wonder if there isn't something else—some other piece of advice the pro can offer to all us "provolones"—and of course there is.

"I hate to say this, but I see a lot of poor grips," he says of the hundreds of pro-am rounds he's played over the years. "It's the start of every instruction book. Every history book says something about the grip because it's vital. It's one of the few things all teachers seem to agree on."

One of the most common maladies he sees is people gripping the club in their palm instead of their fingers. "There's an extent to how far you can cock your wrist that way, but down here," he says, sliding the club closer to his fingertips, "it'll just go."

It somehow figures that this is what it comes back to for Crenshaw. Perhaps no golfer in the past half century has, in all aspects, been more of a purist. And no single element of the game is more basic than the grip. In this age of flash and dazzle, the answer for Crenshaw lies in golf's primary fundamental: the grip.

A day after our talk, the promise of the first two rounds evaporates as Crenshaw shoots 76 in the final round of the Alliance Championship and falls from 7th to a tie for 31st. He will continue to try and work with what he has and not become infatuated with the success of others, but it must be getting harder for this man for whom it used to be so easy. He will take his shag bag and head to the other end of the range somewhere else next week, hoping that golf's John Travolta has at least one more comeback left somewhere still inside him.

Chapter 10

JOHNNY MILLER

*"It's not so important what you accomplish in life that matters,
but what you overcome that proves who you are."*

Johnny Miller is a study in irony.

Northern California born and raised, he owns a house in the Napa Valley, an area renowned for producing some of the world's great wines. Yet, Miller doesn't drink, never has. He is known as a candid, sometimes harsh critic, but he is also one of the most sensitive and humane people you will ever meet. And for all his Hall-of-Fame success—he once won eight tournaments in a single PGA Tour season—his titanic struggle and utter helplessness at one point in the game may be just as historic.

Miller has always been tough to figure out, even for Miller himself. Five days before the final major of 1976, he had to withdraw from the PGA Championship. He'd broken his wrist trying to pop a wheelie on his Harley— just four weeks after winning the British Open.

"You'd think a good little Mormon boy wouldn't do all

that stuff," he says, "but I just did too many fun things. I was always screwing around."

His role as an opinionated television commentator has made him famous among those who've never even seen him swing a club. The very week we sit down to chat, the Golf Channel is running a program that highlights some of the more memorable things Johnny has had to say over the years. Miller's words not only have weight but possess a certain adhesive quality. They tend to stick in a communications environment, where, as ESPN's Chris Berman is fond of saying, you can't really get too hung up on what you've just said, because right now "it's somewhere around Pluto."

Another planet might be where some players would like to send Miller. There was the time in 2004 when he said that Craig Parry's swing "would make Ben Hogan puke." Parry then went on to win the tournament by holing out a six-iron from the fairway in a play-off over Scott Verplank. But number one on the Golf Channel countdown is Miller's suggestion that Justin Leonard was playing so badly at the 1999 Ryder Cup that he needed "to just go home and watch it on TV." A day later, Leonard sank one of the most memorable putts in golf history against Jose Maria Olazabal.

"Sometimes I'll look over there, and I'll see Johnny's wheels turning at a feverish pace," says NBC's Dan Hicks, Miller's broadcast partner since 2000, "and he'll actually take his hands and close his mouth as if to say, 'I really want to say something here, but you know what? It's best

I don't.' It's a physical maneuver where he takes his hands and pinches his lips as if to say, 'Not today!' "

What's lost in the outrage about what Miller *says* is likely a true appreciation for what he *did*. There are players who have won more Tour events and more majors, but for a brief time he was extraordinary. After turning professional in 1969, he missed a total of six cuts in his first eight seasons. During the 1974 and 1975 seasons, he won 31 percent of the Tour events in which he played. And, of course, there was that 63 at Oakmont in the final round to win the 1973 U.S. Open.

"During that time period, he hit nothing but good shots and a lot of great shots," remembers Andy Martinez, Miller's caddy during his glory years. "He used to say that confidence is knowing that even your worst shot is going to be good. For him back then, it was just like degrees of good."

But from that lofty perch, there was a long way to fall. After winning the British Open in 1976 at Royal Birkdale—his eighteenth career victory and second major in eight years—something changed.

"I just got burned out," Miller says. "I had sort of accomplished almost everything that I had ever wanted to in golf. Right then and there, I could have walked away."

We are sitting in a rented house in the Tucson foothills, both of us in town for the World Golf Championships—Accenture Match Play Championship. The sun is setting on the other side of the picture window, and the horizon is pink, with only the cactus silhouettes looming quietly. Miller and I are talking about his worst times in golf: his slumps. That we should be doing so here in Tucson is ironic. Majors aside, it was here in Arizona, a generation earlier, where he earned some of his most dominant wins. They called him the Desert Fox. He won the Tucson Open four times, including the 1975 event by nine strokes. In 1980, he told *Golf* magazine: "I had a stretch there for a few years where I played some golf that bordered on Twilight Zone. I'm not saying I did it for a very long period of time, but even so, during that span I played some golf that I think is unequaled. I can remember that I was literally getting upset that I had to putt. I was all over the hole.

"Hitting the pin and having the ball bounce away. I just couldn't wait to step up and hit the next shot to see how close I could come."

But by the end of the 1976 season, Miller's life had unalterably changed. He and his wife Linda already had four children at home, all under the age of six. And Miller started a new hobby: real estate. That fall, he bought a piece of property in Napa.

"It was a hundred-acre ranch," he says now, wistfully, recalling the first of perhaps fifteen ranches he has since bought and restored. "It was beautiful. Had some vineyards in the front and had a lot of old buildings that had been run down and kids were using for party places; all the windows were broken. And it had an old tennis court and an old water tower. And the main house had burned down. It was supposedly haunted."

Miller says he was totally consumed with owning his first big piece of property. He bought a tractor with a front loader. He hired a crew to help him, and then he set about restoring the property, using not only the equipment but his bare hands as well.

They started in September, and by January, he says, the ranch was immaculate.

"But in the process of doing that, I'd gone from 175 to 194 pounds, and I still had a thirty-one-inch waist. I looked like I was ready for the NFL."

All the while, he never touched his clubs.

"I mean, no golf," he says. "I'll never forget going to Tucson at the start of the year [1977], and I was the defending champion, and I went out to hit balls five to eight days before the tournament, and it was like there was no club head there. It was like the clubs weighed nothing."

Miller's new muscle-bound physique created a significant problem. He could still hit his irons effectively, but his driver, he said, "went to the dogs."

"I was blocking the ball right. I was hitting the ball like thirty yards right—a lot like Tiger Woods hits them—but he gets away with them better than I did. I didn't have a short game. The probable reason why I was in a slump is I had no chipping game at all. I was a pretty good sand player but a terrible chipper and pitcher of the ball."

So now, the player who had dominated the game over the past two years not only couldn't hit a fairway but was miserable. Every chance he got to play *the game* he loved forced him to leave *the ones* he loved. It was a toxic combination. He tumbled from 2nd to 48th on the money list and the year after that to 112th.

Then came the injuries and the surgeries: his knees, his shoulder, his gallbladder, his back, his wrist.

"I was just a mess," he says. "I looked good—you know, I looked like a model—but I was really banged up. On a flight, I'd fly first class and then go in the back and find three open seats and lie down because the pain was so bad. I couldn't ride in a taxi cab unless I could lie down in the back seat."

Miller became so desperate about his game's dysfunction that he characterized himself as the king of the WOOD keys (Works Only One Day). He tried painting a dot of his wife's nail polish on his putter's grip, the better to focus on the pendulum-like rhythm of putting he desired. During one tournament, a voice told him to close his eyes while putting. Another time a voice beseeched him to only watch the hole.

"I'm full of weird things," he says.

Miller stood on the edge and came within a hair of parachuting into the comfortable life of corporate outings and course design. But something stopped him.

"I started thinking about my kids," he says. "And I

started thinking: what kind of an example is this that I'm setting for them?"

He started to think about something he believes came from the scriptures: *It's not so important what you accomplish in life that matters, but what you overcome that proves who you are or what kind of man you are.*

"And I was thinking, my word, I've never overcome *anything*. How can I quit now? What are my kids going to think?"

The question haunted him, so he buckled down. After a month of no results, something strange happened. He was all alone one evening on the twelfth hole of the Silverado North Course when a voice—again—told him what he was doing wrong. He had a sense he was hanging back instead of moving through the ball. Perhaps *that* was why the ball was going right.

"If I'd had a teacher I was working with at the time, he probably would have seen it right away," he says.

He dropped a half dozen balls to the turf as the sun set and tested his theory. It worked . . . kind of. "I was still hitting it right, but only about fifteen feet," he recalls.

But he remembered something Lee Trevino had once told him and added that into the equation: "If you're hitting it bad or choking, just hit it low. It doesn't have time to get off line."

There in the northern California twilight, Miller had manufactured a way out of the abyss. It was what he termed "a low ugly fade—a push-cut."

"All of a sudden," he says, "I've got a shot that was kind of an anti–choke shot. I could get on those holes that had out-of-bounds and water that were freaking me out, and I had a shot I could play. I had a foundation I could stand on."

Miller decided he would quit once he was able to show his kids he had gotten his game back, but then he started having a second career. He won events in four straight years from 1980 to 1983. In 1981, he won twice. It wasn't quite the incandescent brilliance he had radiated in the mid 1970s, but he was once again among the game's elite.

"I was still able to make a living out there," he says, "but it was excruciating." As much as he had figured out a way to get from the tee to the green, once he had a putter in his hands, he was nearly helpless. At age forty-two, he stopped playing full time.

———————

There are no simple answers with Johnny Miller. The slump that knocked him off the top of the game was caused by a body that changed, a body that then became broken, and a spirit that suffered when he couldn't be with his young family. But another factor also derailed him. He changed equipment.

"In 1976, my manager convinced me around the British Open that the three best players in the game were Weiskopf, Miller, and Nicklaus, and he said there's not enough room for you three in this little company [McGregor]."

So Miller signed a lucrative deal with Wilson. He played a different ball and gave up the irons he'd been using "forever."

"It was the biggest mistake of my golfing career," he says.

At his best, if Miller had a calling card, it was how deadly accurate he was with his irons. They used to say he wanted his distances in half yards instead of yards, because he was so dialed in. Chi-Chi Rodriguez was convinced that Miller's irons were imbued with some type of strange magic, but, ironically, they were actually technological relics.

"My irons were World War II irons," he says. "They were stainless [steel] because you couldn't use chrome, which they put into the war effort. They were made in the mid 1940s."

The irons that strafed Oakmont and desert courses from Palm Springs to Tucson were thirty years old. Players today would use thirty-year-old clubs just as soon as they would drive a thirty-year-old car. After Miller signed his new equipment contract, he gave the irons to Rodriguez as a gift when Rodriguez stood in for him at an outing. Sadly, soon after, they were lost.

But as much as Johnny Miller is known to one generation as a once-in-a-generation talent, to another he's primarily the man who fuels countless chat rooms and then drops a match to set that fuel ablaze.

"I think 99.9 percent of it is Johnny," says Dan Hicks, "but to a certain degree, he knows the audience is expecting something out of him, and he knows that he has to rise to a certain level every telecast. In other words, he's got to give them something so they can look to their buddy and say, 'Did you hear what Johnny said!?'"

It's not just on the air, though. Two weeks later, Miller is getting ready for the final-round telecast of the Tour's Tampa event. He looks up from his work and asks me how my book is coming.

"It's interesting," I say. "I'm learning a lot."

And then, without asking, I become an audience of one.

"There's no game that's ever been invented that exposes someone's choke point like golf," says Miller. "It highlights all your weaknesses, mental and physical, and choking can really be part of a slump. It's the most interesting thing about the game.

"And it's so funny: people always say to me, 'How can you talk about that stuff?' Well, how can you *not* talk about it?"

I laugh, because it occurs to me he's right and because to Johnny Miller it all must seem so terribly . . . ironic.

Chapter 11

DAVIS LOVE III

"Try less hard."

As the rain clouds roll low and ominously over the Redstone Golf Club at the Shell Houston Open, the staff's day-end duties are taking shape. Wave after wave of mowers and rollers and all manner of turf-grooming vehicles emerge from the maintenance barn and fan out to repair the course from this day's play and make it ready for another. As each machine leaves the compound, it rolls past a sign of the times: a silent column of motorized wealth parked bumper to bumper on the course's back lot.

"We love this thing," says Davis Love III of his $1.7 million motor home—one of seven parked in the lot at Houston. "It's got everything we need."

And indeed, the forty-five-foot Featherlite H3 has just about every luxury you can imagine: three flat-screen TV sets, satellite dish, washer-dryer. It is among the rewards for two decades of impressive consistency and success on the PGA Tour. Before an ankle injury ended his 2007 season and necessitated surgery, Love had finished 16th or better on the money list in fourteen of the previous sixteen years. His career earnings totaled more than $36 million. With these numbers, it's hard to imagine he has ever struggled in the game.

"Slump? What slump? I've never had one," he'd e-mailed me when we first started to discuss the subject. As we sat in this Taj Mahal on wheels earlier that season at Bay Hill, Love chuckled at the self-deprecating sarcasm of his e-mail and its obvious absurdity. No one who plays golf is immune from slumps. Love says he's had four or five "rough patches."

"1994 sticks out because that's when I should have been winning a bunch," he says. "Maybe I was really trying way too hard."

As the 1994 season began, Love was a rising star. Not yet thirty, he'd won five times in the previous two seasons, including the prestigious Players Championship. But after starting the year by almost winning in Hawaii and then stringing together a handful of other solid finishes, he nose-dived. He missed seven cuts, including the Masters and the PGA Championship, and didn't record a single top-ten finish after March.

"I remember being so frustrated the last few months of '94," he says, "and I was ready for somebody to shake me up a little bit, I guess." Unfortunately, the person he needed most wasn't around to do the shaking.

If anyone ever arrived on this earth destined to be a golfer, it was Love. Not only was his father a highly regarded teaching professional, but Love was born only hours after his dad arrived home from the 1964 Masters, where he'd shared the first-round lead with Arnold Palmer, Gary Player, and two others.

Davis Love Jr. was soft-spoken and old school. He played golf for Harvey Penick at the University of Texas, and he taught his own son in the same uncomplicated manner that Penick had taught so many others.

"One day my dad was hitting seven-irons [at a practice green] and Harvey walks up and goes, 'Davis, get me some five-irons on that green.' And Dad goes, 'Well, coach, I can hit seven-irons on that green.' And Harvey goes, 'Get me some five-irons on that green.' And then he walked away. So Dad started hitting five-irons, and he had to hit them real smooth and real easy, and he said it just hit him. That's how you get your rhythm back is hitting them real slow."

It was hundreds of practical lessons like this that formed Davis Love III's golf education—an education augmented with an almost Buddhist philosophy. "Let your attitude determine your golf game. Don't let your golf game determine your attitude."

The quote is from *Every Shot I Take*, a book of Davis Love Jr.'s observations about life and golf put together by Davis Love III with the help of Michael Bamberger. The source material was culled from piles of legal pads and scraps of paper penned by Davis Jr. and saved by his son in a big wooden filing cabinet.

But in November 1988, Davis Love Jr. died when the small plane in which he and three others were flying crashed on the way to a golf instructional outing. His son was twenty-four and had won his first PGA Tour event only the season before.

"For many months after the accident," says Love in *Every Shot I Take*, "I would wake up in the middle of the night, and tears would be streaming down my face. My sobbing was uncontrollable."

Love had lost not only his father but his best friend, his teacher, and the person most closely attached to what, outside his family and his faith, meant the most to him: golf. Nonetheless, he went on to have a decent season the following year, working under the tutelage of Jack Lumpkin and Todd Anderson, men his father had mentored. But it wasn't easy, and it didn't get any easier.

"They try to help, and they do a good job," says Love, "but they still go back all the time and say, 'Your dad said do this' or 'Your dad said do that.' The emotional family side of it, you don't really ever get over that; but the golf side of it, it still goes on."

Sometimes, even today, Davis Love Jr.'s continuing

presence sneaks up on his son, especially now that his own son, Drew, is becoming a player.

"I got a lesson from my dad last Friday," says Love, stating the presumably impossible.

Lumpkin was teaching Drew, and the lesson had been recorded on DVD. As Love watched it on a computer he heard familiar and useful words.

"Drew," said Lumpkin, "what you've gotten yourself into the last month, I can't fix in one day. Your grandpa would have told your dad to swing a six-iron 30 percent, and then 50 percent, and then 75 percent. And then he'd make him hit a driver 100 yards, and then 125 yards, and then 150 yards. I want you to do that for a month."

"And I heard that," says Love, "and I said, 'Oh, shoot, that's what I have to do.'"

Back in 1994, the problem was a little different.

"At the time I thought, 'I'm really good,'" says Love, "'and I'll just keep doing it.' I won a lot of money and won some tournaments, and it was just coming to me for a while."

But then, all of a sudden, it wasn't. Lumpkin confronted him with the unpleasant truth: Love was coasting. He had gotten sloppy with his swing and his practice habits, and he needed to get back to work. So every day Lumpkin had Love meet him on the range at nine in the morning for two hours. It was like he was a kid again. And gradually, Love started to see results. The following year, he won at New Orleans, and the week after that, he had a dramatic second-place finish at the Masters. Love finished sixth on the money list that season with an impressive nine top tens.

"It always seems to boil down to some fundamentals and then putting in the time," says Love. "Tiger always used to say it a lot: 'I just have to go out and get some reps.' Like he was lifting weights."

Talk to any golfer long enough, and it's inevitable the subject of Woods will come up. But many players, Love included, think that most people miss the point.

"The general public should be amazed at what Tiger Woods does," says Love, "but they shouldn't try and use his clubs or his swing. They should try to figure out how to concentrate like that. I'm not interested in swinging like Tiger—I'm interested in putting like him—but I want to know why he outthinks everyone. How he approaches it."

Certainly technique is important, but Love thinks that golf is primarily a thinking man's game. He uses basketball, one of his favorite spectator sports, to explain how sometimes people think too much.

"It's like shooting free throws," says Love, who got Michael Jordan started on his golf addiction when they were undergrads together at the University of North Carolina. "You have so much time to think. But if you're coming off a pick and shooting a jump shot, you just shoot it. You have to not think about results—just play."

And sometimes people don't think enough.

Recently, NBA superstar Lebron James started working with sports psychologist Bob Rotella to try and get better from the free throw line and from beyond the three-point arc.

"He's just not quite as confident [with free throws and three-pointers]," says Love, who's worked with Rotella for years, "as when he's flying through the air and going to smash it into the backboard." James's plan wasn't to try and learn how to shoot three-pointers or free throws; it was to "learn" how to be more confident. That would be the difference.

Love concedes that while all this makes sense to him, there are no universal truths for golf. Many people struggle with the game or go through a slump when a personal issue causes a problem, but that's not been the case for him. One of the most productive periods of his career came amidst a time of extraordinary pain and personal turbulence. In 2003, Love was having perhaps the best year of his career. By the middle of April, he'd already won three times. But when he came home from a tournament in early May, he found out that his brother-in-law, who worked for the family's golf course design business, had been embezzling money from him. Jeff Knight was married to Love's wife's sister and worked for the Love family, doing just about anything from fixing whatever needed to be fixed to driving people to the airport. He also managed the family's personal finances.

On May 11, as Love and his son were getting ready to

go on a hunting trip, Knight came to visit and confessed he'd been systematically stealing money from Love over a period of time and was being investigated by the FBI. Five days later, Knight, a veteran of Desert Storm, disappeared. As Love told Bob Verdi for an interview that year in *Golf Digest:*

"I had a bad feeling, so I drove to his fishing cabin. He had backed his big Suburban up to the house and run a pipe from it to the exhaust on his car, and blacked out all the lights on the car so nobody would think it was running. He put a brick on the accelerator. He had taken a six-pack of beer inside with him, plus two bottles of pills, then sat in a chair and shot himself. He had planned it for three different ways to kill himself in case one failed."

Love's world was turned seriously upside down. Not only had he been violated by an employee and family member (close to a million dollars was stolen), but now his wife's sister was a widow, and his niece and nephew no longer had a father.

But a few weeks later, Love went back to work and finished tied for 7th in Washington. After missing the cut at the U.S. Open, he completed the year in extraordinary fashion. He finished tied for 4th at the British Open, won in Denver, finished 3rd in a World Golf Championship event, tied for 5th at the season-ending Tour Championship, and then capped it off by shooting 63 in the third round and winning the Tiger Woods invitational tournament in December. "It's almost like when I'm distracted," says Love, "and not putting a lot of pressure on myself, I get better and better."

In fact, the season after his father died, Love actually improved his standing on the PGA Tour's money list, the overall gauge for success. After Davis Love Jr. was gone, his words seemed to resonate particularly clearly in his son's thoughts, and through the years he has found them to be the perfect lesson when he hits one of his "rough patches."

"Try less hard," Davis Love Jr. used to say. His son finds that to be perpetually useful advice and sees its proof on country-club putting greens across the country.

"You're getting ready to play," he says he tells people at clinics, "and you throw three balls down on the green. You're talking to your buddies and you hit that first forty-footer. What does it do? And they all go, 'It goes in!' and I go, 'Yeah, because you didn't aim it, you didn't try, you didn't care, you were distracted . . . you just putted one.' And then, you gather up your balls and you get three feet from the hole, and you go, 'I gotta make some three-footers before I go out there, and you keep missing. You get all frustrated."

Try less hard. That brings into focus one of golf's great paradoxes. If you're going to break out of a slump, you actually have to apply yourself and try *very* hard, but it must be in the right place: on the range, not the golf course itself. It's a unique but necessary talent to be able to think technically—until you get to the first tee. Tom Kite is a master of the art.

"He could ask five different guys on the range—three pros, a caddy, and a marshal—to help him with his swing, and then he'd go out on the golf course and just grind it out. Hit the ball wherever it went, then just go get it. He'd get the most out of a round of anybody. Then he'd go back to the range and he'd change everything and think about something different. He can turn it off and turn it on better than anybody."

Kite was one of the first people Love looked to for advice when he came out on Tour in the mid-1980s. It's no coincidence that he learned from Harvey Penick—another connection for Davis Love III to his father.

"I still feel like I need my coach, my dad," he says quietly as we sit talking on his bus.

It has been twenty years since Davis Love Jr.'s plane crashed and ended his life. It didn't end his teaching career.

Chapter 12

JUSTIN LEONARD

"I really had to kind of make things my own. I had to own it."

In what is undoubtedly both the greatest paradox and absurdity of this book, Justin Leonard and I sat down to talk about slumps and struggles one afternoon in the lobby of a Houston hotel where a tattoo and body piercing convention was taking place. There is perhaps no player on Tour less likely to be found among the crowd gathered that week at the Sheraton hotel than Leonard, who for many years had an endorsement deal with the very emblem of preppyness, Ralph Lauren, and once told *Golf Digest* that he organized his sock drawer. Oddly enough, it might have been Leonard's inability to embrace his uninhibited, more creative side that not long before had landed him in trouble—deep trouble.

For the world's elite players, a slump can be a subtle thing. A loss of consistency, a lack of confidence, a general malaise. On a fast track, little things will leave you a lap behind before you even have a chance to tune the radio. But sometimes the issues aren't so little, and the slump is anything but subtle. That's where Justin Leonard found himself in the late summer of 2006.

"There are times when you're playing so well, you know success is winning your golf tournament," he says. "Anything less than that is probably a little disappointing. And at times, top ten is a success. At times, making the cut is a success."

After starting the year with two top tens in his first three events that season, that's exactly where Leonard found himself: struggling to make cuts. Eight times in his final twenty events, he failed to make it to the weekend. He accumulated the worst scoring average of his career.

But as bad as it was, it wasn't catastrophic.

Not yet.

"I knew I wasn't playing very well," he says, "but after the season, that fall, I played in the Shark Shootout [an unofficial event where golfers play in two-man teams] with Scott Verplank, and we lost in a play-off. So I thought, 'Okay, if I could take that little piece of momentum and do something with it at the beginning of the year, I'll be headed in the right direction.'"

Regardless, Leonard was experiencing a first bump in the road in a career that had showed nothing but promise, even though initially you might not have picked him out of the crowd as the one you'd be watching on SportsCenter.

"My first memory of him was that he was very, very small." Randy Smith was then an assistant at Royal Oaks Country Club in Dallas, where Leonard's family had a membership.

"He was about seven years old," says Smith, "and he walked into the shop, and I thought, 'His mother really needs to feed him more on a regular basis.' Very small, spindly arms, little bitty legs, cute kid, always looked like he was up to something."

The boy soon grew, but his talent mushroomed in a disproportionate, almost mutant fashion, and when he was thirteen, he won his first significant junior title at Indian Springs in Broken Arrow, Oklahoma. On the drive back to Dallas, Leonard excitedly called Smith to tell him all about it.

"And then, about three and a half hours later, the bag-room door flies open," says Smith, "and here comes Justin with this big old trophy. It was really neat to see his reaction to winning, and competing, and succeeding, but the coolest thing was when he turned around to walk away and go home. It was the weirdest thing I've ever seen out of a kid. He stops and says, 'And now I want to know *more.*'"

Smith, who was about to become the club's head professional, felt not only enormous pride but extraordinary pressure, too. In one instant, it dawned on him that if Leonard—a player of infinite potential—was going to become a better player, Smith would certainly have to become a better instructor. "At that moment right there is when I probably started my teaching career," he says. The fortunes of the two were immediately tied, and the closest of relationships started to take shape.

"Randy was like a second father to him," says Amanda Leonard, Justin's wife.

Teacher and student got busy "getting better," and the partnership—on which, with one interruption, the meter is still running two decades later—became crisply productive. Leonard had extraordinary success at the highest levels of amateur competition. At the University of Texas, he became the first player in Southwest Conference history to win the conference individual title during four consecutive years. In the course of his amateur career, he won the NCAA individual title, the Southern Amateur, the Western Amateur, and the U.S. Amateur. His senior year at Texas, he won the Haskins Award as the nation's top collegiate player.

After graduating from college he immediately dove into the professional game by way of sponsors' invitations, the discretionary wild cards that tournament organizers can extend to those whom they choose. In only his third week out, he finished third at the Anheuser-Busch Golf Classic. By the end of the year, Leonard had accomplished a rare feat: he'd made enough money to earn full playing privileges on the Tour for the coming year and thereby avoid one of the most intimidating rituals in all of golf, the PGA Tour's qualifying tournament. At Q-School, instead of playing for a living, talented hopefuls find themselves playing only for the *right* to play for a living.

"I would almost classify it [avoiding Q-School] as a tournament victory," he told *Golf Digest*'s Mike Stachura in August 2000. "The pressure towards the end of the year was weeks long, not a week long."

In a short time, Leonard's professional success started to approach that which he had found in the amateur game. He won the Players Championship and the oldest and most venerated title in the game: the British Open.

There were players who were bigger, and those who hit the ball farther, but Leonard had developed an extraordinary short game. With a wedge in his hands, he was deadly.

But in the late fall of 2006, as Leonard hit his first real rough patch as a developed player, all that success and precision seemed like a distant memory of a different person.

Like many people after a bad day of work, he went searching for comfort. For some, it's an easy chair and a hard drink; for others, it's the self-flagellation of a day at the gym. For Leonard and his young family—at the time he had three children, all three years old or younger—it's time spent at their vacation home in Telluride, Colorado.

"It's totally his escape," says Amanda. "He doesn't pick up a club; he doesn't think about it. He doesn't watch the Golf Channel. He skis every day."

The Leonards spent the New Year's holiday in the mountains and gratefully waved goodbye to 2006, which had turned out to be Justin's worst full season on Tour in thirteen years as a professional.

"We thought, we're going to go up there [Colorado] for three weeks and just totally get away from the game," says Amanda. "And then to come back in the beginning of '07, when you think that was kind of the answer and then to go out and miss six cuts in a row, it's like, 'Holy cow, we've got a bigger problem on our hands.'"

From the Bob Hope Chrysler Classic, the third week in January in Palm Springs, California, to the Pods Championship in Tampa eight weeks later, the extent of Justin Leonard's golf consisted of the same routine: two disappointing rounds followed by a lonely plane ride home on Friday night. One of the most consistent players on Tour had become totally lost.

"I'd never really been where I was that year," Leonard says of the start of the 2007 season. And for a moment, the fastidious golfer at the tattoo and body piercing convention doesn't seem so out of place. He too had suffered great pain in pursuit of a means of expression.

"I was trying to make myself believe that I was playing okay," he says, "because it's hard to go out there and play with no confidence. And sometimes you have to try and trick yourself a little bit. It doesn't mean I thought I was playing great, but I thought, 'My game's pretty good on Tuesday and Wednesday; why can't I get that to Thursday and Friday?' I had some brutal Friday nights."

Probably none worse than Friday, March 2. Earlier

that day, Leonard had bogeyed two of his final four holes at the Honda Classic in West Palm Beach, Florida, and missed advancing to the weekend by two strokes. It was his fifth consecutive missed cut. About half an hour after she figured he'd finished his round, Amanda Leonard called her husband on his cell phone.

" 'Where are you?' I said. And he could barely speak. He said, 'I'm in the parking lot of Whole Foods.' I grew up in West Palm Beach, so I knew exactly where he was. He was about halfway home from the course, and he pulled off to the side of the road in his car, and he was crying so hard he couldn't drive. Sitting there all alone. I think that was probably his lowest point."

The same golfer who a decade earlier had fearlessly shot 65 in the final round to win the British Open found he had become a totally different player without even realizing it. Instead of playing to win, he was playing not to lose. When you're playing your best, he says, "You don't think about any consequences." But Leonard's slump had turned him timid and cautious.

"It's so easy to slip into those bad habits," he says, "and it's so hard to get out of them. It doesn't make any sense to me, but it's true."

As is often the case, the lowest point is frequently the turning point, and so it was for Leonard. Sports psychologist Dick Coop was in town and staying with Ian Baker-Finch, the CBS Sports commentator and former British Open champion who had gone through his own catastrophic slump in the mid-1990s. That horrible Friday of the Honda Classic, Leonard took his first step back to golf's land of the living by planning a house call the next day to see the doctor.

"He could see," says Leonard, "that I had gotten way too technical with things: golf swing, putting stroke, reading putts. He even talked to me about how I walked on the golf course."

Coop wanted Leonard to try and emulate Fred Couples, to loosen up and try to be less intense. Of course, asking Leonard to dial back his intensity while playing golf is like asking a leopard if he can do something about those spots.

"It's just trying to get away from all those technical thoughts," says Leonard about the essence of Coop's message, "and you know, just holding the steering wheel too tight. I just had to get to where I let it go."

The pair did several drills to try and restore Leonard's feel and confidence. The following week in Tampa came another big step. After missing the cut by two strokes, Leonard made some dramatic changes. He knew that no one was likely to have a better handle on his problems than the man who had known his game from the very start, but there was a complicating factor. Six years earlier, at the end of a relatively indifferent season, Leonard had decided he needed new counsel in an attempt to make his game more contemporary. So he walked into Randy Smith's office the week after he returned from a trip to Europe and told him he was going to change instructors.

"That was one of the hardest things I've ever done," Leonard says quietly. "I felt like I had to make some changes in my golf swing, and I just felt like Randy, because we'd worked together for so long, and he'd seen the success I'd had [with that approach], that he wouldn't be able to really rip the Band-Aid off and not start over but go in a different direction."

"That was no fun," says Leonard about going to see Smith and telling him that he planned to start working with Butch Harmon.

"Did it hurt?" I ask Smith, as always on the range between lessons at Royal Oaks on a windy day.

"I'd be lying if I said it didn't. It was a tough time. But you can't blame someone for wanting more. You can't blame a guy for wanting to get better."

Leonard won four tournaments with Harmon looking after his swing, but none in almost two years. So this time, Leonard made the difficult call to Harmon and an emotional one to Smith

"I said, 'Bud, will you please, please take me back? I'm not playing any good, but do you want to come help me figure this out?'"

The two talked for a few minutes, and something was immediately apparent to Smith.

"I wasn't talking to the kid I'd known. I was talking to a different individual. I was talking to somebody who had seen the other side. Somebody who was pretty deep in despair. I was definitely talking to a grown man."

Smith had been keeping an eye on his old friend by way of television broadcasts and felt he knew exactly where his "miss" was. He told Leonard not to do a single thing with his golf swing until he got to Bay Hill the following week. Then, there was a very simple set of instructions: "No matter what the circumstance, *work* every shot. High, right to left. Low, left to right. Vary your height. Create something on every shot you take. There is not going to be a 'stock' shot."

"Oh, jeez," Smith remembers Leonard reacted.

"Just do it," Smith commanded the player who now represented Nike.

"The reason I wanted him to move the ball around was because that's the way he won tournaments. He could hit a 60-degree sand wedge in there fifteen or twenty feet off the ground from eighty-five yards, have it hop three times, and make the ball stop on a dime when he was playing in the NCAAs. That's a shot that other people wouldn't even dream of hitting. And he did it with so much control, it was ridiculous."

Using his "new" instructor's advice that week at Bay Hill, Leonard finally made a cut. It was a start. He took the following week off and went back to Royal Oaks so Smith could have a close look.

"When you struggle, things go haywire," says Smith. "His grip was pathetic. I've never seen a grip on a Tour player . . ." his voice just trails off and stops. "And it was leading to things in his swing. And the setup wasn't anything like I would have liked it to be."

Smith wanted Leonard to get back to the way he used to "control the ball through spin or lack of spin to get at the pins." They worked together on the basics for two and a half months.

And while Smith was revamping the technical aspects of Leonard's game, Leonard himself got busy with some of the other things he felt were holding him back.

In an off week that March, he and his wife went to visit Lanny Bassham, a Dallas man who'd initially made a name for himself as an accomplished target shooter. After failing to win at the 1972 Olympics, Bassham developed a system to help him exercise more mental control. Four years later, he won a gold medal in Montreal and has been teaching his system of Mental Management ever since.

During two eight-hour sessions, among other things, Bassham talked about how people sabotage themselves. How it's not uncommon to migrate back to a level that you might have become accustomed to occupying.

"It's not like you to make a cut right now," Amanda Leonard says of the voice she figures her husband was hearing during his miserable early season trudge, "so your subconscious moves you back into the box where you think you should be. After all those missed cuts on the West Coast, he was finally going to make a cut, and

I swear, it's almost like he bogeyed subconsciously, because it wasn't like him right now to be making it. He had been playing great, and then it was almost like, 'Oh my god! I'm going to make a cut.' It's something you don't even realize you're doing."

Bassham also had Leonard not only analyze the state of his game, but write down his observations.

"Nothing negative," says Leonard. "All in solutions and answers, meaning 'Tomorrow I need to putt a little better. I need to work on this.' Not 'I didn't putt any good.' Just no negative thoughts whatsoever."

From March until September, he wrote in it every day: "kind of like a daily affirmation," he says.

Between Coop and Smith, along with Bassham's help, there was a lot of information to process, but all the good advice in the world is useless unless it truly has meaning. That realization, in the end, may have been what helped Leonard the most.

"I really had to kind of make things my own," he says. "I had to take whatever Randy or Coop was telling me, and I could go out there and tell it to myself over and over, and try and do it, but until I really understood it, and I believed in it myself, it was somebody else's."

Things started to get better, and then in the late summer and early fall of 2007, Leonard committed himself to loosening his grip on the steering wheel—to "trying less hard," as his good friend Davis Love III might suggest.

He took his first two-week break of the season and told himself, "I'm really going to take ten days off and not touch a club, and when I come back, I'm just going to be totally committed to whatever I'm working on. Even if it's the wrong thing, at least I'll believe in it."

He came back at Turning Stone in upstate New York—an event absent most of the Tour's big names, who had already ended their seasons—and finished tied for 13th. Two weeks later, he moved on to the Texas Open, and with a score of 19 under par, including a 64 and a pair of 65s, Justin Leonard won for the first time in more than two years.

Had he encountered this career turbulence earlier in life, he doesn't think he would have been able to find his way out as efficiently as he now had. At age thirty-five, he was a totally different player from the young hotshot who set the world on fire. But more importantly, he is a different person. First there is his heightened commitment to Christianity, an awakening inspired by his wife.

"I relied so heavily on my faith," he says, "and my wife. It was hard on her. She kept on saying, 'How badly do you want this?'"

And as is the case with many players, children have also leavened his outlook on the game. "They don't care how I play. I mean they care how I play, but they don't define me by that. And I used to define myself by that."

Justin Leonard and I are standing on the driving range
green at Torrey Pines, two days before the start of the 2008
US Open. Three days earlier in Memphis he collected his
twelfth career win—this one in a playoff over Robert Al-
lenby and the reigning Masters champion Trevor Immel-
man. His slump is a distant memory.

"Yeah," he jokes. "It's probably because I'm talking
about it."

Leonard isn't planning to get a nose ring any time
soon, or a tattoo. But he might be more willing to mix
the argyles and the whites in his sock drawer, and he certainly doesn't white-knuckle the steering wheel the way
he used to. His worst time in golf helped him find a better
way in life.

"How much do you learn from winning a golf tournament?" he asks. "I mean, you build confidence, and
maybe there are shots here and there, but you really *learn*
when your back is up against the wall."

Chapter 13

GEORGE H. W. BUSH

"The next one is going to be the good one."

When it comes to work, I consider myself ob-scenely fortunate. For a good part of the year, my "office" is a golf course. My days are spent under the sun watching men and women (and yes, even kids) do things I only accomplish before somebody shakes me out of a deep slumber. If I had a dollar for every time someone said, "You have the world's greatest job," my kids wouldn't need a college fund. And it's not only *watching* great players. I've played more than an occasional round during my spare time on the road. When people ask me how much golf I play, I have a simple answer: "Half as much as I'd like to and twice as much as I have a right to." Among all those days playing, I have counted many privileged and memorable rounds.

I once played nine holes at Isleworth in Orlando with Mark O'Meara and Tiger Woods. As I was about to tee off, I heard a cart screech behind me and then a voice in a stage whisper cackle, "Man, I've been waiting to see *this* for a long time."

It wasn't bad enough that I was playing with two major champions. Now a third, Lee Janzen, had ramped up my anxiety level.

My drive was straight enough (read: not lost), and my primary memory of the day was Woods's pride in his new golf cart, which had more and better speakers than my living room. Both players made me feel entirely comfortable throughout the round. My guess was that they'd seen action considerably worse than mine often enough in pro-ams.

And then there was the time I was hitting balls on the range at the Tradition Golf Club, Arnold Palmer's extraordinary Palm Springs–area club, while I was in town covering the Bob Hope Chrysler Classic. It was late afternoon, and the sun was just starting to disappear behind the Santa Rosa Mountains. The range was nearly deserted except for one other man hitting balls at the opposite end. I noticed that somebody was watching him, but they were too far away for me to see anything more specific. I was swinging well, and the crisp late afternoon air and the promise of a perfect desert evening combined to make a wholly tranquil moment. How could things possibly get much better? I hit a good shot that arced up over the mountain tops and then dropped lazily down when a voice behind me said, "Nice shot, young man." It was Palmer, with a sweater wrapped around his shoulders and a cocktail in his hands. Moments before, I had wondered how the day could possibly get any better. Now I had an answer.

But the most memorable day I've ever had in golf came in the spring of 1997. I was doing a story on the history of presidential golf for the upcoming U.S. Open at Congressional Country Club outside Washington, D.C., and I'd requested an interview with George Herbert Walker Bush. Instead, I was invited up to Kennebunkport for not only a sit-down with the forty-first president but also a round of golf. We met one morning at an oddly familiar site. How many times had I seen the president (and later his son) sitting in a golf cart here at the Cape Arundel Golf Club course near the family's vacation home at Walker's Point? The foursome was myself; the president; Ken Raynor, the club's professional; and Mark Plumber, a local amateur of some accomplishment (he'd once lost to Tiger Woods in the semifinals of the 1995 U.S. Amateur). Bush showed up on the first hole with a tee dangling from his mouth and immediately announced that since he wasn't familiar with my game, the bet would only be "one way" and for a dollar (I was going to argue?).

Raynor and Plumber were his regular cronies, but I was a little unsteady on my feet. The two buzz-cut fellows in dark glasses who materialized wearing coats that were strangely bulky for June were a further reminder that this was hardly going to be an ordinary round of golf. Mr. Bush hit his tee ball. "Reload," he announced with disgust before it even landed.

A "breakfast ball" was allowed on the first hole, but he played every stroke as it lay—often with great frustration—from that point forward. As is the custom with the Bush family, we played with dispatch, finishing the round in just three hours. I would learn that for a man often described as a blue blood, there is no more regular fellow than George H. W. Bush.

"If you go to dinner with him," says his close friend Jim Nantz of CBS Sports, "he's never going to take the choice seat at the table. He's going to make sure you have it. He's going to fight you for the worst seat. It's kind of upside down."

Throughout the course of our round, Mr. Bush offered a running commentary of his own play, sarcastically calling himself Mr. Smooth. "Now here's a shot I'll bet you've never seen," he said. "It's the under-the-tree shot. Of course, I've got to find the ball first."

It would have been a wonderful day even if I had played horribly, which I didn't. I shot 83. Mr. Bush struggled. A few weeks later, I received a note from him along with my winnings, which I had asked him to autograph.

"Jim," it said, "here's your buck back. My golf, believe it or not, has sunk even lower."

George H. W. Bush has a charming talent for self-deprecation, but that day was a reminder that even the most powerful and important men on earth, should they play golf, aren't immune from slumps.

It is more than ten years later and I am sitting in the former president's office in Houston on a dreary January day too inhospitable for golf. The month before, Mr. Bush endured a back operation to mitigate the constant pain. The previous year, he'd had his second hip replacement.

"I'm on the DL," he chuckles. "I'm re-retired from golf. Again."

Bush can't really put his finger on any particular golf slump he's had over the seventy-plus years he's been playing the game, although he admits there have been many. Once, in his thirties, he got his handicap down to 11. In 1949, he won the Cape Arundel Club championship, but on this day, he characterizes the current state of his game as "horrible."

"But I don't worry about that anymore. I just like playing."

"What do you think it says about a person how they deal with their struggles on a golf course?" I ask him.

"That's pretty much the way you deal with your struggles in life, I think. There's always going to be problems, but the quest is excellence. You stay with it and try to do what you can to improve."

He shows me the pictures he's just received that morning from Amy Mickelson: snapshots of her and her husband Phil, along with Davis and Robin Love and Justin and Amanda Leonard from a trip this past summer to Kennebunkport, where the former president annually entertains his many friends from the PGA Tour. He used to engage in spirited matches with the pros who traveled north to Maine, but not so much anymore.

"Well, I've really gotten to the point," he says, "where it's so bad I want to give up the game. But I can't quite do it. I just love the game."

It's hard to think that a golf slump is real adversity for a man like George Herbert Walker Bush. Adversity is your torpedo bomber crashing into the Pacific under Japanese attack during World War II, and knowing that should you survive in the shark-infested waters—which your crewmates didn't—you'll likely be savaged by the enemy if captured. Adversity is declaring war as president in 1990, when the country hasn't been engaged in formal hostilities since Vietnam. Adversity is losing a child to leukemia when she is only four. But for the forty-first president of the United States, whose father and grandfather were both presidents of the United States Golf Association, golf is a game that has been an important part of his life since he was a small child. And it's a game that also provided one of the most anxious moments of his life.

Bush had been asked by Tiger Woods to hit the ceremonial opening tee shot at Woods's inaugural July 4 PGA Tour event in 2007. The tournament honored the military, and thousands of servicemen and women showed up to line the fairways. But confidence was not high for the former commander in chief. He was in a slump.

"I talked to a million people in Wenceslas Square in Prague when they were honoring the Velvet Revolution," he told Woods, "and I'm more nervous now."

Bush summoned all his concentration, made solid contact, and produced a respectable shot.

"And afterward," he says, "I just felt like a million bucks because of the anticipation, the worry, the nervousness—and then it worked."

"How does your dad handle adversity on the golf course?"

It is January 2007, and I'm sitting in the White House library, a small room on the ground floor of the residence, chatting with the most powerful man on earth about the least important thing he'll have to think about this day.

"Pretty well," says the forty-third president of the United States, who has himself broken 80 on occasion but has given up playing the game while the country is at war because of his concern that it might appear frivolous. "Particularly with me, because he understood that he needed to set an example. If he started firing clubs, I'd fire two clubs. If he broke his putter, I'd break all my clubs.

"The interesting thing about adversity on the golf

course is that you can't hide. You have to confront it. If you get the yips, there's only one way to deal with it, and that's to keep hitting golf balls until you get rid of the yips."

This, though, is where the two Bush administrations part company. In terms of policy, the elder Bush agrees, but the practical application has been an issue, and perhaps the reason he's endured his many slumps.

"Didn't practice," says 41. "Didn't get out there and do what my dad did. Didn't do what good golfers now do. All these guys, they go out and hit bags of balls."

At the PGA Tour's Shell Houston Open in 2007, Mr. Bush and his wife were riding on the course with Paul Marchand, a gentlemanly teaching pro who has been a close friend and teacher of the former president since he moved back to Texas in 1993. At one point Mr. Bush started to sneeze repeatedly. "You know, Mr. President, it's probably because we're right by the driving range," Marchand pointed out.

"I'm allergic to practice," says the former president. "I break out in hives."

Bush's own formula for dealing with golf's challenges isn't based in any of the usual technical remedies. It's something far simpler, something he's used in the face of many types of adversity throughout his life.

"He just has this tremendous sense of optimism," says Marchand. "The *next* one is going to be a *good* one."

"You think something that simple can really be effective?" I ask him.

"Absolutely. Your positive frame of mind on the golf course is one of the most important things you can have. It's going to help you avoid having slumps, and it's going to make slumps shorter." And in the Bush approach to golf, optimism has a companion and essential swing thought.

"He's fearless," says Marchand. "I just marvel at it."

At the November 2007 rededication of the George Bush Presidential Library and Museum in College Station, Texas, the eighty-three-year-old former president sky-dove in for the proceedings. Jumping out of a plane at 13,000 feet is one thing, but facing the truly scary things in life is quite another.

"Seeing the water and changing to an old ball. Seeing the out of bounds that's left and trying to hit it right. We never see the flag. We never see the middle of the fairway; we never see the target because we're so afraid of failure," says the other member of Bush's golfing "cabinet," Ken Raynor. He's the head pro at Cape Arundel, who's known Bush and played golf with him for three decades.

"I think the president is not afraid of failure because he keeps things in balance. He's out there to have fun. Everything else is secondary, and there are no real consequences."

"He's kind of like a combination of your grandfather

and your ten-year-old son," says Davis Love III, a frequent Kennebunkport guest. "They want to do everything, and they want to have fun."

And in fact, my mind wanders back to that wonderful round at Cape Arundel ten years earlier.

"You don't remember me talking to you about the power of the Federal Reserve today, do you?" he asked rhetorically that day.

No, I didn't. We talked golf and put all our energies into one goal: enjoying ourselves. I remember that by the end of the day I'd shot my best score ever.

Hmmm.

Golf is an odd pursuit. Maybe the man with the least pure skill is the one with the greatest command of the game.

We're back in Bush's Houston office now. A cane rests by the chair, and you know the former president chafes at his need to use it.

"If you want my philosophy on the game, you're going to have to ask other people," he tells me.

Well, how about some advice?

"I could only give you advice I haven't followed," he says. "Never, never give up. And I forget when Churchill said that. Things can be horrible one day, and, just miraculously, you can hit the ball the next. That's true with me, even though I'm really bad. Don't give up when things are really bad for you."

I thank him. We shake hands, and I walk out of the office. I can't help thinking that the advice he claims he hasn't heeded is the very wisdom he'll be chanting when Mr. Smooth gets the urge to bust out of his present slump and the days in Houston become more hospitable once again.

Chapter 14

ARNOLD PALMER

"Slow down. What's your hurry?"

I n a modest white clapboard house at the end of a sleepy cul-de-sac in Latrobe, Pennsylvania, sits the most unlikely corporate headquarters you will ever find. Arnold Palmer Enterprises occupies a ranch-style home on this block that might well have been clipped from the pages of *Suburban Living* magazine circa 1962. It's the same block where the company's founder and chairman has lived since 1958.

Five days a week, for most of the year, that's where you'll find Donald "Doc" Giffin, sportswriter for the Pittsburgh Press from 1953 to 1961, PGA Tour Media official from 1962 to 1966, and, for the past 41 years, the man who has been the keeper of Palmer's legacy. Want to know where and when Palmer won his first big-time professional event? That's easy enough to find in the record books or on Google (1955 Canadian Open), but Giffin can give you what you might not find elsewhere.

"I think probably the most interesting thing about that tournament," says Giffin, "is that not only was it his *first* win, but in one way, it was his *best* win. He shot 64-67-64 and 70 for 265 (23 under par). That was the lowest score he ever shot in a seventy-two-hole event."

You'd figure then it would be all downhill from there. Of course, nothing could be further from the truth. Palmer went on to win sixty-one more times on the PGA Tour. He won seven major championships. But it wasn't just that he won tournaments; it was *how* he won them. And how he lost them, too. Palmer was a swashbuckling, go-for-broke package of charisma with the forearms of Popeye and a thousand-watt smile. Jack Nicklaus was the machine whose performances were as dependable as a Swiss clock. When he had a lead, he rarely let it go. Palmer was, in a way, much more entertaining. Although it might not always have been a prudent strategy, his foot never left the accelerator. He was going to either win, or crash and burn trying. It quickened the pulse just to watch. People seemed to like him because he was what we secretly hoped we could be: fearless. He had "balls." It was often said that men wanted to *be* him and women wanted to be *with* him. But it wasn't only the talent and the sex appeal. This man who counted presidents and kings as close friends had the common touch, and it wasn't a disingenuous affectation. He still lives in Latrobe.

More than one writer over time has observed that Nicklaus may have been the best golfer of all time, but Palmer was the most popular. In fact, to this day, he can look into a crowd of hundreds of fans, and at the end of the day, each person might go home and swear the man was smiling directly at him or her alone.

In the late 1950s and early 1960s, no golfer was more successful than Palmer.

"I was winning a lot of tournaments," he says.

We are sitting together on a golf cart as he plays the final hole of the pro-am in what has come to be one of his few remaining competitive outings: the Father-Son Challenge staged outside Orlando each December near his winter home at Bay Hill. Befitting his status—he's known in golf as The King—organizers have bent the event's rules for Palmer, who has two daughters but no sons. He plays with his enormously talented grandson, Sam Saunders, a member of Clemson University's golf team. Palmer struggles with his game but soldiers on and obliges every single autograph request. There's a reason people still ask.

Between January 1960 and May 1963, Arnold Palmer won twenty-five of the eighty events he entered. He had fifty-six top tens. He missed a total of two cuts. He was the Associated Press Athlete of the Decade for the 1960s. But in May 1963, something went wrong.

If you're the best player in the world, a slump has a different dimension: think losing your ball right, instead of just plain losing your ball. Still, this loss of control—for no apparent reason—is just as deflating. If you're accustomed to swinging a golf club with a surgical precision that allows you to feel confident about a 220-yard shot over water, maybe a slump means you miss the green.

That was the point at which Palmer arrived that spring. Here was the man who is said to have created the twentieth-century golf boom in the United States—the man who influenced the man who *taught* Tiger Woods—feeling a little helpless, tired, and indifferent (see, it doesn't only happen to us mortals). What did he do?

"Whenever he was concerned about his game and felt he was slumping," says Giffin, the man who's watched Palmer for half a century, "his solution was to come back to Latrobe and let Deacon watch him."

Milfred Jerome Palmer, "Deacon" to his friends, was a no-nonsense son of Youngstown, Ohio, who chose to make a living under the sun, although not in the glamorous way that his oldest son one day would.

In the 1920s, he found work as a laborer, helping to build a golf course commissioned by Latrobe Electric Steel. Eventually Deacon would sign on as the greenkeeper, and much later, when the club couldn't afford both a greenkeeper and a golf professional, he assumed that job too, having picked up some pointers from the local Scotsmen who had taught golf in and around Latrobe.

"He got to be a pretty good teacher," says Giffin. "He didn't teach many people who weren't members at Latrobe, but if there was somebody promising from the area, you can bet they'd come by."

In September 1929, Arnold Daniel Palmer was born and literally grew up on a course that was something of a sibling to him: it, too, was Deacon's product. As his father sat atop the noisy red tractor that both tamed and manicured the hilly nine-hole layout, young Arnold rode between his legs. Years later, Arnold not only bought the course but had the tractor restored and preserved as a monument to his childhood and what his father had built.

"Deacon thought he was crazy to buy this place," says Giffin. "The country club business isn't exactly a big money-making proposition. But, of course, I don't think Arnold bought the club to make money. I think he bought it for his dad."

Deacon Palmer was the only instructor Arnold Palmer would ever have. He put a club in his son's hands at the age of four.

"The first thing he ever taught me was a good grip, getting a good grip on the club. And, of course, today people still talk about my grip and the fact that it looks like my hands were melted on the club, and that's something I take great pride in. But he showed me how to grip it and just said, 'Now go hit it, boy.'"

By the age of eleven, he was beating the other, much older caddies at Latrobe, and at seventeen, he won the first of five Western Pennsylvania Amateur championships.

Deacon Palmer didn't yell and scream, but his son always understood exactly what he was being told. It was based on a few fundamentals and was not extremely technical.

"He had a temperament and a way of talking to me about my game," says Palmer, "where it really wasn't an instructional thing. It was more like 'What are you doing; why aren't you confident?'"

So in the spring of 1963, after finishing tied for 9th in defending his Masters title, he hit what he considered to be an uninspired patch: tied for 9th in Texas, tied for 2nd at the limited field Tournament of Champions, tied for 44th at Colonial. It was a stretch that might have been fine for many; in fact, Palmer stood 3rd on the money list, but given what he thought he was capable of, it wasn't good enough.

"I was very tired," says Palmer. "I played every week for a lot in a row up until May, and I just needed to get home. I was fatigued, and I didn't get that way very often. But this time I didn't feel good. I lost some of my strength. I had a fatigued golf swing. It didn't have the zip in it that I prided myself in having."

Anybody who's ever played this game has their own idiosyncratic flaw. Something they've had to fight—maybe for their entire life—that returns to rattle its chains time and again.

"The thing I always did that was very bad," says Palmer, "was I got too quick. I got anxious, and when I was talking to my father, that was the first thing he always made me think about: getting my rhythm. Slowing down and being deliberate when I was hitting the shots, particularly in stress situations where the pressure was on and I needed to pull off a good shot. And that was one of the things that helped me probably more than any other single thing: just slow down, think about it, take the club away deliberately."

Palmer came home to Latrobe that May and did what a lot of us do when we struggle with our games: he laid down his clubs and did something else.

"I drove a bulldozer for a couple of weeks working on the golf course," he says. "We were building Latrobe Country Club, the second nine holes. I needed to do something different, so I just dug dirt and helped on the golf course."

And then, after a couple of weeks, with his mind clear, he started hitting balls again—slowly.

On June 16, after an unprecedented five weeks away from the Tour—his longest hiatus to date—Palmer returned to road-test his therapy. He won three of his next six events and lost in a playoff to Julios Boros at the Open.

"I felt revitalized. It was one of the really good times in my life," he recalls. "I felt like I could make whatever I wanted to happen happen."

For the rest of his career, Palmer applied the same therapeutic formula whenever he faced a slump: he would come back to Latrobe, find a quiet place on the corner of the range, and seek his father's counsel. Even after Deacon Palmer died in 1976, his son came home to find the answers.

"I always went back to him whether he was there or not," says Palmer. "And I would go by myself on the practice tee and think that he's standing there telling me what to do. I would think about what we'd worked on in the way that he would say it. And I would work that way. By myself . . . for hours."

Back at the Father–Son now, Palmer's group has reached the green. Over more than half a decade of professional golf, he has played in hundreds of pro-ams with thousands of partners. He has seen it all.

"I think the most important thing is that people get anxious," he observes, "and they think the faster they hit balls and the more they go out and hit golf balls, the sooner they're going to get it back—and that's just the opposite. What they should do is go back and practice, yes, but think about it. Do it more deliberately than they ever have in their life, and I feel that they will recover much faster in the game than they would any other way."

"So slow down a little bit?" I ask, thinking that perhaps the King might have an answer for a commoner like me.

"Slow down your personality," he says, "Walk slower. Slow down everything you do."

With that, he pats me on the back and heads off to the other side of the green to take his turn. He hits a sleek little chip to six inches, smiles, and responds to the ever-present and adoring army that seems to track his every move, and then he turns to me and winks.

Slow down, I think. Take your time in everything you do. Good point. I'll have to remember that.

Chapter 15

DOTTIE PEPPER

"Forget the stuff that's bad," she says, echoing her father's advice,
"and go do a little something of what you're good at."

Fear is a terrible thing; for a nervous flyer at 30,000 feet, for an underachieving employee waiting to see the boss, and certainly for the golfer of modest means who has more than just her game to lose.

"I remember thinking to myself 'I've lost it,' and if I can't play, they're going to take my scholarship away."

"Would you say you were panicked?" I ask Dottie Pepper, winner of seventeen LPGA titles, including two major championships.

"Total panic," she says.

"Tears?"

"Yeah, like I said, total panic."

From the safe distance of twenty-plus years, Pepper thinks back to the first time she realized a golf swing could be slippery and mean, as easy to figure out as calculus with a hangover. She had been a prodigy, mentored by two extraordinary men: her father, Don Pepper, a former professional baseball player, and George Pulver, a soft-spoken central New York version of Harvey Penick.

"He [Pulver] was very much into simplicity and not over-analyzing," she says. "It was 110 percent fundamentals, and he never let me read the instructional articles in golf magazines. You can read all the human interest stories and where to go to play, and about all the golf course architecture, but you cannot read the stuff about how you're 'supposed' to swing the golf club, because he thought that too much input was a disaster. I worked with him until the time I had to tell him where the ball went."

Despite winning the New York State Women's Amateur at age fifteen, Pepper got a grand total of one recruiting letter—from Texas Christian University—in high school and ended up with a scholarship only because the letter *she'd* written to the coach at Clemson, which didn't have a women's team, was passed on to the coach at Furman, which did. But the winter of her junior year at Furman University, Pulver passed away at age eighty-seven, and Pepper soon started to develop a nasty hook—that is, when she wasn't cold-shanking it. So there she was that fall more than two decades ago, standing with uncertainty on the eighth tee at the Pat Bradley invitational in Key Biscayne, Florida. After a brief lifetime of nothing but confidence with and mastery over the game of golf, she was convinced she'd forgotten how to hit a golf ball. This was a girl who'd needed a special waiver

from the state in high school because the five years of var-
sity golf she played was on the *boys* team, the last three as
the number one player.

"It was a par five, dogleg to the right with nothing but
mangroves and water right," she says uneasily, recalling
her first brush with a slump. "You played out of a shoot,
and I stood there, and my last thought was 'I can't hit
this. I don't know how to get this ball in play.' "

Somehow, she was able to safely bail out with "a big
old shot to the left." But the effortless game of her youth
had suddenly and cruelly turned into work. She was ter-
rified. "I got home from that tournament and called my
dad, and he drove in an ice storm with my sister from
New York to South Carolina."

"I think it was the morning after Thanksgiving," says
Lynn Pepper, her mother, "and they just nonstopped it
from upstate New York, which to Greenville is about seventeen and a half hours."

"We drove in, and she was on the range in the rain,"
says her dad. "I think she had her notes from Mr. Pulver,
but she was in such a panicked state she wasn't concentrat-
ing on them. I'd never seen her like this. She didn't even
want to put her hands on the club, she was so scared."

For two days, Don Pepper worked with his daughter in
the rain and then got back in the car and drove straight
home. Dottie was "fixed" . . . at least enough to make
her first overseas trip and play in the United States–Japan
matches a week later.

"I never hit a shank," she says of her play in the matches. "I won two and tied one. It wasn't pretty, but I got it done."

But Dad's fix, she admits, was a Band-Aid. When she got home for the Christmas break, the real work would begin, because home was where things seemed to make the most sense.

———

Ten and a half months out of every year, Saratoga Springs, New York, is a quaint and modest burgh of Victorian homes on the southern edge of the Adirondack State Park. "From New York City, you drive north for about 175 miles," Red Smith once famously wrote in the *New York Times,* "turn left on Union Avenue and go back 100 years."

Life here is friendly and quiet and sane. Then comes the summer meeting of the thoroughbreds each August at the Saratoga Race Track, and things change. Almost a million people descended on Saratoga for the summer meeting in 2007 and wagered more than $123 million. The track is the oldest existing thoroughbred facility in the country and has been staging its six-week schedule since the Civil War. If it's not the racing, it's the performing arts center or the seventeen public mineral springs. In summer, Saratoga is still quaint; it's just hard to find a parking space. It seems it's been that way forever. George Washington is said to have "taken the cure" at Congress Park in the naturally carbonated waters that surge through the local limestone and shale.

It made perfect sense, then, for Don Pepper, a former first baseman in the Detroit Tigers system, who had come back home and struggled in a handful of businesses, to rent out his house come August to the race crowd hungry for housing. It would pay for a lot of things, but most importantly, in the early 1980s, it would provide the down payment on a dream—one that wasn't even his.

On July 29, 1981, an estimated 750 million people worldwide watched as a kindergarten teacher married the man in line to be the next king of England. Even though the Peppers had two young girls, the fairytale wedding was of only marginal interest in their household. It was the weekend's second most important event behind the New York State Girls Junior Championship, which Dottie won. Earlier that summer, she had won the State Amateur. She was fifteen. Her parents had always insisted on balance in life, but now they might have to rethink things.

"All I could think of," says Lynn Pepper, "is, 'How is this going to happen?' I would lie awake in the middle of the night worrying and say, 'God, if you've given her this kind of talent, please help us open some doors, because we just don't have the money to do this.' The one resource we had was our home."

At that point, Don says, the decision became automatic.

For the next four years, the Peppers rented their home for Saratoga's summer meeting, sometimes getting as much as $4,000. They moved into an apartment above the barn at Lynn's parents' place, and Dottie hit the road. But first there was a cautionary note from a man who was a local phenom but in the end got only three major-league at-bats—and no hits—in a seven-year professional career.

"My father's theory was always 'If you think you're good here—let's see—you're *one* of fifty states. There's fifty of you.' And he said that was the lesson he'd learned coming up through baseball. If you think you're good *here*, there's lots of other *heres*."

Don Pepper's daughter eventually barreled through one "here" after another. The game seemed easy until she realized that was just a child's fantasy. During those two days in the rain at Furman, Dottie Pepper learned a world about adversity and what to do with it. Even though her father was at his best a six handicap, he knew things that would serve his daughter a lifetime in a sport where, as George Pulver had been fond of saying, "It doesn't have to be perfect to be good."

"I think she was psyched out," Don says now with a laugh. "I can remember I said to her, 'You didn't go from good to bad overnight, so you just need to try to get your *mind* back to where it was.' I had gone through it [in base-ball], but I really didn't have anybody to talk to to stay positive. I tried to tell her that even when she had a bad round of golf, to take good things from it. Everything has some positive in it. I think because of the down times I was able to convey how to be more positive to her."

That was the mental part of the lesson, but there was a physical corollary: you need to develop a "go-to" shot. When things are going badly, you need to have a parachute.

"For me, that was a soft draw," she says, "and to do that, I had to make sure my legs drove first, so it was going back to the fundamentals—again—that Mr. Pulver taught. He always thought that leg action led upper body action. He would always say, 'Start from the bottom.'"

Dottie Pepper went on to have an impressive career, and it would be more than a decade before she hit another significant pothole. But this time, things were different. She had her "go-to" shot. That high draw provided the safety net to relieve the panic that had disabled her game before. But she had something else, too. Although George Pulver had died when Dottie Pepper was only twenty, he'd left a road map for her to find her way out of the wilderness when she was lost.

After every lesson, and also after the Sunday afternoons the two had spent together watching golf on TV, Pulver would leave a letter in the Peppers' mailbox. Pecked out on his old manual typewriter, it might highlight the essence of what the two had worked on or discussed that day. Or it might have little to do with golf, instead focusing on life's bigger picture and things the old pro thought were worth contemplating. Time and again over twenty years, she'd pull out the letters and read.

"It was part of what I did to get out of a slump. I read Mr. Pulver's letters."

They were usually about a page long, sometimes only a paragraph. The first letter was placed in the mailbox on Worth Road on March 15, 1980, when Dottie was fourteen years old; the last came five years later and bore the signs of a man with failing sight and diminished mental agility. She still keeps them in a notebook in her office.

"Everyone must find his own way of attacking the golf ball," he wrote in March 1981. "I have witnessed the bent left arm of Vardon. The majestic sway and lurch of Hagen. Trevino, who appears to be beating an animal on his downswing. Lopez with her sudden starting away wrist cock. Yet these titans of golf past and present had more:

THEY HAD REPEATING SWINGS.
THE WILL TO WIN.
ENORMOUS CONCENTRATION, UNDER A THOUSAND EYES.
AND FINALLY—THE MOST IMPORTANT SHOT IN GOLF
THE ONE BEING PLAYED."

In his weekly notes, Pulver used words like "felicitations," "canard," and "covetous." He was an elegant, thoughtful man who might be highly technical: "Learn to set the club face with both hands as you step to the ball," he wrote in July 1982. "This is superior and more natural than setting with either hand, and preserves and aligns your shoulder line at the same time."

And from October the year before: "Every time you practice, hit a few casual five-irons. Then pick up your power clubs and try to capture the same pace. The power will come from the longer shaft and arc and not from additional effort."

But on the heels of a technical discussion might come a cautionary note about being slave to such thoughts: "Teachers of golf spend their lives and their energies sorting out theories," he once wrote. "Great players play by feel, not by theories. Do not get too cerebral."

Pulver was an elegant philosopher-gentleman who ended every note by asking to be remembered to Pepper's parents. He was fond of quoting the wisdom of the greats—not only Jones and Snead, but Hemingway. His advice was equally suited for the accomplished and the novice.

"If possible," he wrote in August 1981, "do not play winter rules. Play the ball as it lies, even near the greens. In no other way shall you learn to play tight lies without trepidation."

There were a hundred letters in all, and they came in handy in 1996 when Pepper's nine-year marriage to Doug Mochrie ended. He wasn't only her husband; he was also her coach. It was a perfect storm, and she was a mess.

"I knew I'd really lost it at the Open at Pine Needles," she says. "I missed the cut, and it was the first time I'd ever missed a cut in a major championship."

But it got worse.

"The first thing you want to do is just get in the car and go home, but I couldn't. My mom was coming up to watch me play on the weekend, and *she* had the car. She had to come and get me. That was pretty pathetic," she laughs. "Thirty-one years old and I can't go home. My mom has to come and get me."

Pepper withdrew from the following week's tournament and just, as she says, "got off the train." She retreated to her home in the South Carolina mountains and did two things: thought about George Pulver's words and worked as though she was a teenager back at the "Duffer's Den," the pitch and putt her parents had once owned near Saratoga.

"I worked till my hands bled," she said. "I'd hit balls, I'd chip, I'd putt, go home for lunch, go play nine, and then go back and hit more. It was an all-dayer."

She emerged restored and won four of the next eight events. She beat back the slump by applying two seemingly contradictory concepts: hard work and insouciance.

"Do you think there's any universal fix for a slump?" I ask her.

"It's usually something very basic and something that

repeats quite often, too," she says. "You fall into the same bad mistakes: bad setup, bad grip. Just bad fundamentals.

"I think the average Joes probably take whatever the golf magazines tell them they should know and then over-apply it. For those of us who are lucky enough to play golf as a job, we kind of know what we're looking for, or know what we're looking to feel."

Just like a country club chop, Pepper says her slump that year was because she'd gotten careless with the basics. She knew it right away, so the fix was easy. There was the hard work, and there was the wisdom of George Pulver, but also there was the advice of the six-handicapper who rented out his home to the horse players so his own thoroughbred could reach full gallop.

"Forget the stuff that's bad," she says, echoing her father's advice, "and go do a little something of what you're *good* at."

"Reinforce the positive, huh?" I say.

"Yup," she replies.

The golf swing can be a complicated thing, but for more than a few people who play this game well, the key to success isn't about loading the mind with swing thoughts, but rather emptying it of almost everything except fundamentals, confidence, and determination. It's ironic that one of Pepper's favorite letters from George Pulver recounted an old Scottish tale—one that had nothing at all to do with golf. It came when she felt particularly defeated by the game first invented in Scotland hundreds of years before.

"The tale of Robert Bruce, heroic Scottish king, who won independence from England comes to mind," wrote George Pulver on August 28, 1982. "Three times he assailed the English armies, and three times his brave Scots were driven from the field of battle. Lonely and discomforted, Bruce found himself in a cave. As he sat there with his melancholy, he observed a spider, swinging back and forth, trying to reach the safety of his nest. Three valiant efforts failed, but in his fourth attempt, the spider reached his nest. The story goes, Bruce arose, buckled on his sword, and gathered his scattered minions together. Returning to battle, they drove the English from the field."

Most people are lucky to find one person as a guide through the minefield that golf often presents. Dottie Pepper had two. George Pulver's and Don Pepper's methods were different, but their messages were more similar than they might appear: sometimes we make things an awful lot more complicated than they need to be. Don't think too much; you'll hurt yourself.

Chapter 16

TOM WATSON

Tom Watson is standing in the middle of the fifteenth fairway at the TPC Tampa, playing in another Thursday pro-am on the Champions Tour. As he surgically deposits a mid-iron approach to the middle of the putting surface, it is immediately and abundantly clear he is different from you and me. From a vantage point beyond the ropes, it's principally the rhythmic and effective swing—and, of course, the result—that seems to separate one of the greatest golfers of all time from the rest of us. But step back further in time, and you see that the swing, and what it begat, is simply where the difference begins.

Like many great players, Watson started playing golf when he was very young. When he was six, his grandmother brought him to a skills competition at Mission Hills Country Club in Kansas City, where a twenty-seven-year-old assistant pro knew he was looking at a child who was different from most his age.

"They're all trying to slug the ball, and they're falling all over themselves," says Stan Thirsk, who went on to become Watson's lifelong teacher and friend. "He [Tom] didn't do it. His balance was perfect."

Watson was all of fourteen when he won the Kansas City Men's Match Play Championship. By that time, he'd already been part of a regular Saturday afternoon game with his dad's friends at Kansas City Country Club for a year. And why not? He broke par—on a short course—at twelve. As a thirteen-year-old, he shot 67 at Kansas City. But for all the promise his golf career showed—starting at age seventeen, he won the Missouri Amateur four times in five years—Watson was plainly different from his peers among golf's young elite.

"Golf was not the most important thing," he says, "but it was certainly one of those things I loved to do."

From September to March, he didn't play; he was far too busy. Watson was a guard on the basketball team and the quarterback on the football team, which went 7–2 his senior season.

"We had summer football practice starting in the middle of August," he says. "I played in the National Amateur, and the football coach got a little upset when I asked him to let me out of practice so I could go play golf. 'That's just pasture pool, that's all,' he said."

Watson was wooed by several college golf powers—

Oklahoma State, Houston, and SMU—but instead took a different path. He paid his own way at Stanford because that's where both his father and older brother had graduated.

"Stanford had a budget of $8,000 in their golf program," he says. "They didn't have any money for a scholarship, nor did I ask for a scholarship."

So, on a national stage began the journey of a player who followed his own compass rather than any existing map. When he turned professional four years later, he immediately seemed different from his peers.

"Most of us were just trying to figure out a way to make some cash," says Andy North, a two-time U.S. Open champion and long one of Watson's closest friends, "and if we could win a tournament, great. But I truly think *he* was thinking, 'I could be the best player in the world.' He wasn't unbelievably talented, like some players. He worked his tail off to figure it out. He had an unbelievable will to get it done."

"This man used to get up and go to the golf course at seven or eight in the morning," says five-time PGA Tour winner Bob Murphy, another of Watson's closest friends, "and not come home until six at night."

"I was a ball-beater," says Watson. "I hit more balls than anybody. I'd hit four or five hundred [in a day]."

At first, the strategy didn't really pay off. Watson went his first two-plus years on Tour not only without a win but also firmly establishing a reputation as a player who *couldn't* win because he couldn't finish. Some of his early struggles might have grown from a personality trait that would eventually surface both on and off the course and be a recurring theme in his life. Some called it determination. Some called it stubbornness.

"If he sets his mind to something, it's going to happen," says Thirsk. "No matter how long it takes, he's going to do it. He will not take no for an answer. He won't give in to anything."

"He believed that if the shot called for a cut, he would play a cut," says North, "even though early in his career, he may not have been able to pull it off. There were a lot of times he lost tournaments when he tried to do it the right way, instead of the way that was best for him at the time. But because of that, it made him a much better player three or four years later, because he tried stuff under pressure."

Through three rounds of the 1974 U.S. Open at Winged Foot, Watson held the lead and looked as though he might break through, but a nine-over-par 79 on Sunday famously sunk his chances. Later, in the locker room, he met and was consoled by Byron Nelson. As Watson and I sit talking outside the press room at the Outback Steakhouse Pro-Am almost thirty-four years later, the first thing he mentions about that day isn't the relationship with Nelson that blossomed soon after—a story that for many has come to define his experience there. What he first talks about is the specific nature of the problem he encountered that Sunday, one that would haunt him for much of his PGA Tour career.

"Ball going straight right all day," he says.

Just two weeks later, he won his first title at the prestigious Western Open. A year after that, he won the British Open. Two years later, the floodgates opened. Between January 1977 and July 1984, Watson won thirty-three PGA Tour titles, seven of them majors.

"He was Tiger Woods for five years," says a fellow pro who played with him during that time period.

But he wasn't perfect. The flaw that plagued him that Sunday at Winged Foot would revisit him more than occasionally. He had, however, developed and sharpened a way to compensate.

"He'd hit it wild and just go find it and figure out a way to make a par," says North, "and that's a great ability."

"It became a joke on Tour for a while," says Murphy. "He would drive it and beeline right into the woods."

Watson was fearless and supremely confident, but the factor that enabled him to play successfully, and seemed to differentiate him from everybody else, was his short game. As a young teen at Kansas City Country Club, he used to go out and play by himself and drop a handful of balls in different locations around every green each time he played.

"And then," remembers Thirsk, " he'd go and choose the club, determining the lie and whether he had to pitch it, or bump and run or whatever." The result was a multifaceted short game that would serve him well for many years.

"I've always been able to score with my short game," he says. "I remember one time playing Harbor Town with Gardner Dickinson. I shot 71 that day and hit five greens."

"When he was really good," says North, "it was absolutely astounding. If you go back and look at films of him winning tournaments, he'd make putts, and when he missed them, he'd have an eight-footer coming back and they'd *fly* into the hole. It was the ultimate confidence in putting."

This was a man who was clearly different from a lot of others, and it wasn't only the way he played golf. In 1990 he resigned from Kansas City Country Club, the place where he had grown up and learned to play golf, when a Jewish applicant was denied entry for no apparent reason. He publicly complained when Bill Murray danced an elderly spectator into a bunker at Pebble Beach, and he sparked bad feelings when, as Ryder Cup captain, he refused to engage in the tradition of autographing the rival team's menus at the gala dinner. In a game where complaining about others behind their backs is the norm, he boldly confronted Gary Player when he thought he had intentionally breached the rules.

"He always tells the truth," says Thirsk, "and if it's going to bother you some, then too bad—the truth is the truth, and that's the way he is. He's not a phony."

Ultimately, though, the type of shots Watson fired that got the most attention were ones like his two-iron from 213 yards to the 72nd hole at Royal Birkdale in July 1983.

"Best two-iron of my life," he told Dan Jenkins of *Sports Illustrated*.

Two putts later, Watson had his fifth British Open title, beating Andy Bean and Hale Irwin by one stroke. There would be three more PGA Tour wins in 1984 and one more in 1987. Tom Watson was thirty-eight years old and seemingly in the prime of a Hall of Fame career. But he would never win another major championship and was about to embark on an unimaginable winless streak, which crossed ten seasons and spanned 140 events.

"Looking back, does that surprise you?" I ask him.

"Not the way I was playing," he says.

Once, Watson seemed different because it looked as if he just couldn't lose, but then, all of a sudden, he became just like everybody else when he couldn't win.

"I always figured I could practice myself into playing well," he says, "and after a period of time in 1984, it wasn't working. I got more and more frustrated, actually to the point where I gave up on myself and gave up on the game."

So he took a hiatus, he says to "alleviate the stress," but that didn't work either. This man, who not long before had made winning seem routine, now finished in the top three just five times in 108 events.

"I didn't like it," he says. "I couldn't accept it. You're trying to do something at the level I'm trying to do it, and you're failing where you've had success before. My career wasn't very much fun."

But the same determination that had once convinced Watson he was right about taking perhaps unpopular positions now compelled him to find a way out of the morass. Ball-beater that he was, he went back to the range again and again.

"It was very frustrating. I just kept doing what I was doing. But I was doing it wrong, and I finally figured out why."

After playing terribly in a practice round at Hilton Head in 1994, and again losing shot after shot to the right, Watson made a dramatic change in his swing.

"I said, 'I am not going to physically swing out to the right anymore.' I'm going to feel like I'm going to swing over the top. I'm going to come so far over the top of the ball with my right shoulder that I'm going to make the ball go eighty yards left."

The divots from the first two shots he hit with his exaggerated new swing were slightly left, but the shots themselves went dead straight. The third ball, he hit slightly thin, but it also was straight. It was 3:15 in the afternoon, and the light switch went on.

"Obviously I had built a flaw into my swing," he said, "and I corrected that flaw."

In the hour or so that Watson and I sit talking, he

often mentions the moment of clarity he would search for whenever things weren't going quite right. Of all times, he had one the week of his most famous win, the 1982 U.S. Open.

"I went into that tournament hitting the ball sideways," he says. "I couldn't find the fairway." But his driving was so wayward, he actually benefited. "I was in where the gallery was walking [where it was flattened down] so I could play," rather than in the heavy rough just outside the fairway's confines. After thirty-six holes, he stood at even par and then went off to the range, where he had one of his "light switch" moments: a realization that his swing needed to be flatter at the top with more unity between arms and body. "I started striping it," he says. He shot six under par on the weekend. The culmination of the week—courtesy of his short game—was a near impossible chip in for birdie at Pebble Beach's par-three seventeenth on the way to a two-stroke victory over Jack Nicklaus. "The shot," as it is known in Watson's circle of friends and family, was voted by a select industry panel in 1996 as one of the greatest moments in golf history.

Watson's epiphany a decade later at Hilton Head was more complicated. His swing change made him realize it wasn't just the swing, as is often the case; it was the setup, too.

"My fundamental flaw was that my ball was too far forward [in my stance]," he says, "and my right shoulder was too low. It wore on me. I just couldn't hit it."

But once Watson made the change, he got "immediate results from it."

"I played well in the tournament," he says. "I didn't win it, but I played well."

He had solved what then appeared to have been his most serious problem, and two seasons later, at age forty-six, he won the Memorial.

"If Tom Watson—from 1975 to 1990—hit the ball like he did from '94 till now," says North, "he would have won twice as many tournaments."

Just as he was correcting one problem, though, another was starting to surface. The two plagues were intimately connected. All of a sudden, the man who could make anything from anywhere, couldn't. And what was worse was that the closer to the hole he got, the hairier it became. It put enormous pressure on the rest of his game.

"Take the seventeenth at TPC Sawgrass," says North of the famous and treacherous par-three with the island green. "If the flag's on the back and you're a really good putter, you won't have a problem just hitting a wedge down to the front there, and if it doesn't bounce up on the back, you know you can two-putt from fifty feet and it's no big deal. You lose that ability to two-putt from fifty or sixty feet, and now you're forced to try and throw it on that back level of that green, where there's a good chance it's going to bounce into the water over the green. It changes the way you attempt to play holes when you're not putting as well.

"There was a time when if he [Watson] hit it [to] fifteen or eighteen feet, there was a chance that he'd make that, but if he missed it, and he had a two-footer, that was as big a question as the eighteen-footer."

Watson had lost his short stroke. It was painful to watch.

"Many, many times I told Gail," says Bob Murphy, speaking of his wife, "sweetheart, if I lose my putting to the extent that Watson did, I don't think I'll be playing. I didn't know how I could do it mentally, but he kept going . . . I think it actually hurt his competitive spirit. How much do you want to take it out there and hit these terrible, terrible putts? A foot, two feet, three feet? The guy was not guaranteed to make it from a foot, foot and a half. How do you get through that?"

Watson says the low point for him came, ironically, at Turnberry in the 1994 British Open. In 1977, the former R.A.F. airfield during World War II had been the scene for one of the greatest head-to-head shootouts in golf history. Playing together over the final thirty-six holes, Nicklaus and Watson went punch for punch. Nicklaus shot 65-66. But Watson shot 65-65 and beat the Golden Bear by a single stroke. Seventeen years later, Watson arrived as a five-time champion who had recently found the answer to his erratic ball striking misadventures. After rounds of 68, 65, and 69, he sat one back and tied for third that Sunday morning and was on the verge of a true breakthrough, but in a short stretch his optimism crumbled.

"I hit it to about five feet at the sixth hole with a two-iron and didn't even come close with the putt," he says, "[and this was] after missing two to three short birdie putts in the first five holes. And that just blew me away." Watson shot 74 and finished tied for 11th, eight strokes behind Nick Price.

"When you're playing badly and you don't win, you have an excuse. But when you're playing well and you're missing too many putts, that's when things get frustrating."

The problem, Watson says, was that on his short stroke, he would for some reason draw the club head back on an inside line. He still battles the problem to this day, although it's not as debilitating as it once was.

"I've tried a lot of things," he says. "Who knows, maybe this week will be different."

And it was.

Playing his final hole in Tampa, he turned reality upside down. Standing in the middle of the fairway with a one-stroke lead, Watson miscalculated the wind and hit his seven-iron approach into the water. After his penalty stroke and drop, he then pitched to within five feet.

Five feet.

Just the type of putt he used to make in his sleep. Five feet. Just the type of putt that had for many years given him nightmares. He calmly stepped up and poured it right into the bottom of the cup. In the next group, Scott Hoch missed an even shorter putt on the same hole to give Watson his second consecutive title in the event after having gone his entire career without a win in Florida. It was the darnedest thing. The shot at which the man had always been money, he screwed up, and the one that for so long now had given him trouble, he absolutely nailed.

"That's one of those putts I've had trouble with over the last fifteen years," he said after the tournament. "I willed it in."

As he moves through his senior career, Watson is once again different. He doesn't practice as much as he used to. His body won't allow it (in October 2008, he finally submits to a total hip replacement), but he still knows the best way out of a slump.

"Every golfer has to adjust their swing to a certain degree through the life span of their golf career," says the man whose spent a lifetime waiting for those moments when the light switch would go on. "Mostly it's because you can work your way into bad habits."

As complicated as the golf swing can be, Watson is yet another pro who cites the simple wisdom of Harvey Penick. If you're playing well, after a bad round of golf, don't do anything. After a second bad round, start thinking about it. And after a third bad round in a row, "You've got to change something."

No matter how different you are, some things are the same for everyone.

Chapter 17

STEVE STRICKER

*"What is perfect? Perfect is whatever you can repeat.
Nobody swings it perfect. Nobody."*

For better or worse, golf is unlike most other sports in that during the course of competition the players are surrounded—often at no more than an arm's length—by thousands of fans. Autograph seeking has thus become a part of the culture. The rope line at PGA Tour events can resemble an overloaded forest of Christmas trees, with the branches replaced by so many arms and the ornaments by items offered for signature. Most pros find a way to oblige—though strategically. Many will reach for an item and then sign as they walk with their heads down. By the time the pro completes his signature, he'll have passed maybe dozens of outstretched hats, programs, and trading cards. He is several yards down the line and looks up and accepts another. By the end of the dance, he has done his duty but has not fallen into the quicksand that this type of thing can become.

One particularly popular gambit is for the player to

engage a member of the media in earnest and dedicated discussion (usually a reporter surprised to have been granted an exclusive audience) as the player makes his way to a "safe" area, thereby giving the pro justification for ignoring the pleading fans ("I'm sorry, I'm doing an interview right now, but I'll be back later after I hit to sign.") In point of fact, there aren't enough hours in the day to sate the demand.

The Tour is like any population, with its varied assortment of both good and bad, but along that spectrum there seems almost universal agreement on Steve Stricker. He leads the league in nice. Watching him the final day of the 2007 season at the Target World Challenge just outside Los Angeles, you see why.

Minutes after he's turned in his card for a final round 70 and a tie for 5th, every autograph request is granted, not a single one overlooked. I count sixty-two signings in eighteen minutes along a fifteen-yard corridor to the putting green. That's one every seventeen seconds, which means he offers not just a signature but a moment of interaction with each person along the way. This is perhaps what he learned from his worst times in golf.

But these are hardly Stricker's worst times in the game. He ends the 2007 season as the world's fourth-ranked player and wins the PGA Tour's Comeback Player of the Year award for a second consecutive year, which is both odd and instructive: his comeback was so mountainous it took two years to complete.

In the dead of winter, the average daily temperature in Madison, Wisconsin, is 17 degrees. Some days it gets down to zero or below, which is really no big deal. It's just the way things are in January. In these conditions, golf, you'd think, is something best enjoyed on television or in daydreams. But there is Steve Stricker in the winter of 2006, in a modified trailer with one side cut out, pounding golf balls into the frigid Wisconsin afternoon and trying to figure out just how his life turned so upside down.

"If it snowed," says Stricker, "they had to plow the range to the side and then get out the yellow balls. Striped balls. White balls in the summer and yellow ones in the winter so you could see them."

The image is almost comical. A three-time PGA Tour winner, a man used to being served buckets of new Titleists (or whatever his chosen brand) just for practice, lashing away at rock-hard "stripers." Every day, for at least three hours, he would break a sweat in this desperate place, far from the comfort and security he'd known for so long. But a slump can make a man do crazy things, especially if he's scared.

"I was wondering if this [golf] was what I wanted to do," he says. "And then I thought: what else *could* I do? I don't know if I'm qualified to do anything else."

He could have been an electrician like his father, or

a carpenter like his grandfather, who in 1941 built the house where three generations of Strickers have lived in Edgerton, Wisconsin, a town of five thousand midway between Madison to the north and the Illinois border to the south. When he was six, Stricker started playing golf and immediately wanted to tag along with his father and his older brother Scott. "That was a big moment in his life," says his dad, Bob Stricker, "when he was old enough and played well enough to go with us."

The Strickers played their golf at the Towne Country Club, at the time a little nine-hole layout no more than a hundred yards from the house. When the weather was warm, Steve was there every day, and before long, he'd turned into a nice little player. But he considered himself more a big fish in a very small pond.

"Growing up, I never thought I was good, coming from a small town," says Stricker. "I didn't play a lot of national major junior events or anything like that. I just kept plodding along in my little area in Wisconsin."

He won the state amateur at age eighteen in 1985, and the Wisconsin State Open a record five times, the first time as an amateur in 1987.

"So I knew I could compete in *that* market, but I didn't really know what to expect when I went south to play against some of the southern guys or nationally."

That wasn't an issue, either. In college at Illinois, he won the Big Ten Conference title a record three times against fields that included players like future PGA Tour winners Ted Tryba and Chris Smith. His junior year, he won the title by fourteen strokes.

The professional game just seemed to be more of the same. After graduating from college in 1990, Stricker immediately earned his card for the Canadian PGA Tour and promptly won the very first event he played as a pro. At the Payless Pepsi Open in Victoria, he beat future British Open champion Todd Hamilton in a playoff. A few years later, in only his second event as a member of the PGA Tour, he finished joint runner-up in Tucson. This was clearly a talent going nowhere but up.

"Every level I got to," says Stricker, "I had some little success right away to give me a shot of confidence knowing that I could play at that level."

But in his third year on Tour came the real breakthrough: two wins, including the prestigious Western Open. He made the U.S. Presidents Cup Team and, playing alongside Mark O'Meara and Phil Mickelson, went 5-0 in the Dunhill Cup matches when the United States team won that title as well. Life seemed impossibly good for Stricker, and maybe the best part was that he never had to wait to call home and share good news. His wife, Nicki, was his caddy.

"I remember how cool it was to be out there," says Nicki. "To be together, just going from place to place and being part of his dream, but then it became both of our dream.

"And I heard it so many times: I don't know how many

people could be married and do what we did. And we had so much fun doing it."

"What was the best part of it?" I ask her.

"That we could do this together."

"Stricker Golf" was truly a family enterprise. Not only was Nicki Steve's caddy, but her father, Dennis Tiziani, was his coach.

"Tiz is basically Mr. Wisconsin golf," says Stricker.

After briefly trying to play the PGA Tour, Tiziani coached the University of Wisconsin for twenty-six years. And even though Stricker was playing for rival Illinois, the summer after his sophomore year he stopped by Cherokee Country Club to see the Wisconsin legend. As the two drove by the pool in a cart, Stricker noticed the very attractive lifeguard.

"Wow!" he asked a bit too enthusiastically. "Who's that?"

"That," Tiziani answered, "is my daughter."

Stricker apologized, but a week later, Nicki called *him*. They were married five years later, and Stricker ended up not only with a bride but with a lifelong swing coach, too.

That day he first met Nicki, he'd stopped by to ask Tiziani for help with his driving, which had grown increasingly erratic. It was a problem that would plague Stricker for years to come, and in fact, even as he was enjoying such dazzling success on the PGA Tour in the summer of 1996, the familiar virus had once again started to infect his game.

Stricker had an extraordinary short game, ranking in the top ten in putts per greens-in-regulation seven times in fourteen years on Tour, which both compensated for and camouflaged the growing weakness. As a driver of the ball he was among the least accurate players on Tour, and he knew it. At the PGA Championship in 1998—a tournament he almost won—he didn't hit a single driver all week, instead opting for the increased reliability and control of a two-wood the handful of times he needed maximum distance off the tee.

"Some things were creeping in [my game] that weren't too good," he recalls.

The year 1998 brought other changes. For the first time since he had become a member of the Tour, Nicki was no longer his caddy. She had gone home to Madison, and on August 31 she gave birth to the couple's first child, Bobbi Maria. Steve held it together for a few more years and in 2001 won the World Golf Championship Match Play Championship—but only, he says, by faking it.

"I could get away with enough bad shots," he says. "I could get it up and down enough times that I could kind of save a round and then maybe throw in a birdie on a par five here or there and kind of fake it through . . . and I think that was wearing on me."

If it had only been a technical problem in his swing, maybe things might have gone the other way, but by 2002, his daughter was in school, so neither she nor Nicki could travel anymore.

"I hated to leave," says Stricker. "Basically, I hated to go on the road. No one was coming with me. All of a sudden, I'm by myself. I leave Bobbi and Nicki at home, and I go and my little daughter's crying when I leave and I'm playing like crap. It just wasn't any fun. And I'm not saying that it all had to do with that, but it just got into my mind and I just didn't want to leave. I just didn't want to go."

In May 2002, Stricker finished tied for 6th at the Byron Nelson Classic. He then went more than two years without a top ten. He finished 189th on the money list, then 151st, and then 162nd. Twice during a three-year stretch he was the single least accurate driver on the PGA Tour. In the midst of it all, he told Gary D'Amato of the *Milwaukee Journal Sentinel,* "I used to hit bad shots—I mean everybody does—but I get up to the tee now and I'm clueless." The bottom had officially dropped out.

"Obviously, my mechanics weren't great in my golf swing," he says, "but a lot of it was mental. I had no confidence. I'd rush through the shot. Almost like an anxiety problem, like, 'I can't wait to get it over with' type thing. All of a sudden you're up over it and it happens so fast and it's another shitty shot. And you're like, 'Where did that come from?' and then you start expecting to hit bad ones instead of good ones, and it's like, 'Here we go again.' Your swing is a product of your mind."

At this point he lapses into a technical assessment of the problem: "It [my swing] got quick. And then I started to get real long and across the line at the top."

"You were searching," I interrupt.

"Totally," he says. "But I didn't know what I was searching for."

He laughs, which is easy to do now, but in December 2005, he hit rock bottom as a golfer, and there wasn't much to laugh about. Stricker had plummeted to 333rd in the World Golf Rankings. For the first time in twelve years, he was forced to go back to the PGA Tour's Qualifying Tournament. No other event in golf inspires the emotions of Q-School.

"That thing is nasty," laughs Nicki, "I would never want to go there."

Q-School is not playing for a living; it's playing for the *right* to play for a living. The difference between success and failure can be seven figures.

"It was humbling, you know. Three-time winner on Tour, and I'm going back to Q-School final stage and don't make it, and now I'm in a position where I have to beg for spots [at tournaments]."

He missed earning his playing privileges by two strokes just weeks after finding out his wife was pregnant with their second child.

So, at age thirty-eight, Steve Stricker went home to Madison, Wisconsin, stripped of his pride with his emotions raw, to try and figure things out. And only when he had nothing more to lose in golf did things get any better.

The reclamation project started with a routine.

"I would work out a little in the morning," he says, "then go and hit balls in the afternoon before I picked up my daughter at school."

And all those days hitting balls out of a three-sided single-wide brought into focus the two things that would need work: his tempo and his position at the top of his swing. The first would be easy, but the second would be painstaking. Changing your swing is like changing the way you brush your teeth. After so many thousands of repetitions, it's instinctive.

"It wasn't easy. I would go up there days, and it would seem to work and my father-in-law would be back there and I would say, 'Is that [my swing] on plane?' And he would say, 'Nope, it's across the line,' or whatever, so you'd think you were making strides and all of a sudden you've got somebody watching, and it really wasn't in the position where you wanted it to be. So some days were good, and some days were bad."

Stricker hit thousands of balls that frigid Wisconsin winter, and gradually the ice began to thaw. He had to wait until the second week of February to get into a PGA Tour event, but immediately there was a sign that he was heading in the right direction: he tied for 14th at Pebble Beach. The same players who for three years had nervously tried to make small talk and avoid mention of their friend's colossal struggles now made a point of finding him on the range to tell him how good his mechanics were looking. Some might have thought the turning point came two months later in Houston when he finished third—his first top-three finish in more than five years—but the most significant event came not in the Texas sun but in the Wisconsin cold.

"I said, 'You know what? I *want* to do this.' This is a game I've played since I was six. So I just have *got* to get better at it, and that's when I started putting in the time. And I had to realize that it [being away from the family] was part of the deal, and Nicki was very supportive. She was like, 'You're meant to do this.' So she's behind me, and Bobbi's a little bit older where she understands I'm on the road and she's coming out to events every once in a while in the summer and she's getting fired up to come out."

And there's one other thing he realized about being away. "I think," says his wife, "he realized that it's not forever."

We are sitting in the now deserted locker room at Sherwood Country Club. Stricker's mere presence in the field—Tiger's invitational is limited to the world's top-ranked players and invited guests—is a sign of just how much his life has changed again. The last two years seem like a blur, but they have been remarkable: sixteen top-tens—three of them in major championships—and a win at The Barclays at Westchester Country Club in the first-ever PGA Tour FedEx Cup playoff event. He is a long way from where he was.

"Does it seem like a bad dream?" I ask him.

"You know what?" he says. "I learned a ton. I look back, and during that stretch of three years, I though it was the worst place in the world to be, and it wasn't much fun. But I learned a lot about myself. I learned a lot about other people. I learned a lot about life in general. I've seen people go through their slumps out here, and they can be brutal. You know, it's no fun for the guy who's going through the slump, and it's no fun for the people he's dealing with. I said, 'You know what? I'm not going to act like that, because I've seen how bad that looks.' I tried my hardest during those three years to be as positive and thankful to other people, volunteers, and treat fellow players with the same respect that I would if I was playing good. What should be the difference if you're playing good or playing bad? I was proud of the way I handled myself. I was proud that I still treated people the same even though a lot of times I was just biting my tongue and unhappy. It was hard.

"You know, golf *is* like life, if you really think about it. I mean, you have your ups and downs in life like you do on the golf course every day. It's just how you deal with them. You've just got to keep a positive attitude about it and believe. Just work a little harder and it will turn around, and the same with life, no matter what it is."

"So then you think for you, lifting yourself out of your

slump was just about hard work and a positive attitude?"
I ask, a bit skeptically.

"Yes," he says, but then he added one ingredient I had
never thought of. "I think sometimes as golfers, we rely on
other people to help us along the way, and sometimes they
throw a lot of information into the pot you might not be
comfortable with. You may not understand it. You're the
guy who has to be comfortable with it the most, so you'd
better work on something you feel good about working
on. And you know what? What is perfect? Perfect is whatever you can repeat. Nobody swings it perfect. Nobody."

So after wandering aimlessly in golf's desert for three
long years before finally kneeling to take a drink, Steve
Stricker's take on the lost years is that they weren't lost at
all. Maybe his prescription shouldn't be such a surprise:
keep it simple, work hard, rely mostly on yourself. It's
an answer rooted firmly in Midwestern values. They are
values that might provide solutions to any one of many
challenges for a kid from a town with fewer people than
the number of autographs he might now sign in a handful
of weeks, whether those problems had to do with hitting
golf balls in a snowstorm out of a trailer, or had nothing
to do with golf at all.

Chapter 18

HAL SUTTON

"Keep your eye on your ball. Your ball."

There was a time in the mid-1980s when the golf establishment became relentlessly preoccupied with a curious exercise. As wide-striped bell bottoms, mutton-chop sideburns, and patent-leather belts faded into fashion obscurity, it became apparent that the greatest player of all time was no longer the force he seemed to have forever been. The Bear was getting long in the tooth, so the golf cognoscenti surveyed the landscape and wondered who was on deck. But the list of "next Nicklauses" became like UFO sightings: frequent and never confirmed.

"Nobody had come along to dazzle the world since him," says Dave Anderson, the Pulitzer Prize–winning sportswriter for the *New York Times*. "I mean, Watson was great, Trevino was great, but they weren't Nicklaus."

And then one day, amidst it all, some thought they might be seeing a few puffs of smoke from the chimney.

Out of Shreveport, Louisiana, came a young man who hit the ball like Nicklaus—and won in the impressive fashion he did, too. He even looked like Nicklaus. Hal Sutton seemed to have it all, and more than a few were convinced that he was the one.

"There are players that, when they hit the golf ball, there's a clacky sound, or a zippy sound, or there's a heavy thud," says PGA Tour veteran Peter Jacobsen. "Nicklaus hit the ball with a heavy thud. Tiger hits it with a heavy thud. John Daly hits it with a heavy thud, and that's how Hal Sutton hit the golf ball . . . very impressive."

Sutton had won the 1980 US Amateur and then, with much expectation, roared into the world of professional golf. His rookie year, he finished a lofty 11th on the money list and won the season's final event, but it was his sophomore season when he went from someone to watch to someone you couldn't afford to take your eyes off of. On his way to winning the money title, he won the Players Championship, arguably the game's most important title after the four major championships, and then four and a half months later, he stared down Nicklaus himself and won the PGA Championship at Riviera in Los Angeles. "I sat in the clubhouse and watched Hal," says Jacobsen, "and he was just tougher than nails coming down the stretch."

In his previous start two weeks earlier, he had gone into the final round of a Tour stop in Virginia with a world of confidence and a six-stroke lead. But Sutton shot 77 that day to finish two behind Calvin Peete, who shot 69. He had matched the largest blown final-round lead in PGA Tour history. "I was just devastated," says Sutton. "I thought I could spot everybody in the world six shots and they couldn't beat me."

Chastened by the loss, Sutton went back home to work on his game. At dinner one night that week, he told his father, Howard, that instead of waiting, as he customarily did, until the weekend, his dad might want to come out this week and see the *entire* tournament, because Sutton said not only did he plan to win the PGA, but he was going to do so after leading from wire to wire.

"And my Dad said, 'You really think you're going to do that?'" remembers Sutton, just twenty-five at the time. "And I said, 'Yeah.'"

And that's exactly what he did. Paired with former PGA champions Lanny Wadkins and Lee Trevino, Sutton opened with a 65 and followed it up with 66. By the back nine on Sunday, he had a four-stroke lead and seemed to be galloping away with the title as predicted. But then in a scene nauseatingly reminiscent of the event he had just coughed up two weeks before, Sutton bogeyed the twelfth, thirteenth, and fourteenth holes.

He stood on the tee of Riviera's long dogleg par-four fifteenth hole and asked his caddy, Freddie Burns, for a towel. "All of a sudden it's hot as hell out here," Sutton told Burns.

"That was a turning point for me," says Sutton, who parred the final four holes to win by one. "To pull it back together and not lose it again, because then I would have been pegged for the rest of my life." If Sutton could have signed on for that to be the worst of his problems, he would have had a good deal, because what he ended up going through was so much worse.

———————

Hal Sutton grew up a child of privilege, the son of a wealthy oilman. As a boy, if there was a sport, he would gladly play it: football, basketball, baseball. "I came in one day," he remembers, "and I told my Dad, 'I'm tired of playing these team sports.' You were so dependent on everybody else doing their job, and some cared and some didn't. I told him I like golf. I'm only dependent on me."

Sutton was sixteen years old and a three handicap that summer when he gave up the other sports. Two and a half months later, he was a "scratch" player and won the Louisiana Boys Junior Championship. "At that point I knew if I worked at it," he says, "I could be pretty good."

It seemed that every college with an elite golf program wanted him. He went for a visit to the University of Houston, where the legendary golf coach Dave Williams took him into the library where the portraits of the school's forty-two All-Americas hung.

"And he said, 'Look at that, Hal,' " Sutton remembers. " 'You could be number forty-three!' And that just didn't have a very good ring to it: number 43. Who remembers number 43?"

So Sutton stayed home and enrolled at tiny Centenary College. With just eight hundred students, it was at the time the smallest school in Division I. "It was kind of like high school," says Sutton. "Everybody knew everybody."

The University of Houston had carloads of first-team All-Americas. Sutton became Centenary's first, and thus far only, golfer to claim such an honor. Before he knew it, he was on Tour and making people wonder if he was the "Bear apparent." In his first five seasons, he won seven times. "Things came pretty easy for me early on," he says.

And—not surprisingly for a young, successful, attractive guy—he lived the high life. He married and divorced three times. As he told *Golf Digest*'s John Hawkins in early 2000:

"When I first started making money, I thought the first thing that would make me happy was a fast car, so I bought a Porsche. The second thing I thought would make me happy was if I owned a house, so I bought a house. The third thing I thought would make me happy was if I bought an airplane, so I bought an airplane. After all that, I finally realized I wasn't going to buy happiness, and I wasn't going to find happiness through somebody else."

And then, as quickly as it had arrived, the magic was gone. Sutton says he was seduced by the twin Sirens of success: complacency and distraction. "At that point I was looking to do everything *else* I could," he says. "I was riding [cutting] horses all the time and doing stuff that was away from golf. I wanted to escape. I really took my focus off of golf and put it elsewhere."

But Sutton says that even if he'd had his focus, he's not sure he could have pulled it together, because "it just wasn't working."

As easy and instinctive as golf had once been, all of a sudden the game was now that foreign and hard. Between 1987 and 1993, not only did he fail to win a single tournament, but he seemed to have lost his game entirely. He was panicked and says he went to see "every major teacher there was to see." In 1992, the man many were touting a decade before as the "next Nicklaus" finished 185th on the money list and missed twenty-one of twenty-nine cuts. "The whole thing was a blur," he says. "Probably every week was an abomination."

"It got so bad," Sutton once told me, "that I was afraid for the spectators. Most guys when they're struggling, they know where they're going to miss it. I didn't have any clue where the ball was going off the tee."

And it wasn't only a parade of golf instructors who got in Sutton's head. "I used to go and play Augusta," he says with clear contempt, "and *they'd* say 'He'll never play good at Augusta because he doesn't hit it high enough.'"

I've met hundreds of athletes who were clearly bruised by the torrent of critical rhetoric a person who lives his life in the public eye often endures. But most, if not all, will turn around and claim they don't read the papers, even though they can quote the articles line by line. Not Sutton.

"So you were influenced by what people were writing and saying?" I ask.

"Oh yeah," he bristles. "It would be like me trying to take over your job. It would be offensive to you for me to act like I could—and even be an authority on it! But I'm letting that sort of thing influence what I'm fixing to do!"

The bottom came in Las Vegas when he sat down at dinner one night near the end of the 1993 season with a handful of statistics to see where he needed to improve. It was not a pretty sight. His best ranking in any of the primary categories was a tie for 95th in putting. He didn't crack the top 100 in anything else. He remembers thinking, "I got so many things wrong I don't know where I need to start."

Sutton chose to turn away from the nationally known instructors he had been working with, preferring to just "wallow out of this myself."

What counsel he did take was from a man not many had heard of: Floyd Horgen, his college coach. Some scratched their heads. "See, if I'm failing," Sutton explains, "nobody thinks I know what I'm doing because I've got *him* helping me. So it's up to me to have enough confidence that he and I will have what it takes to get where we need to go."

The first step was to start playing golf as if he was in a pond and jumping from one lily pad to another—playing from point A to point B to point C. "I tried to hit spots," he says. "I started looking at a bullseye."

"And would you sacrifice distance to do that?" I ask him.

"Oh yeah," he says. "We're living in a world right now where people think distance is a big deal. I'm telling you right now, distance is NOT a big deal. You do not sacrifice accuracy for distance. You get as much distance as you can WITH accuracy."

But Sutton's bullseye approach wasn't only about where to put the golf ball. It was about where to put his energy and thoughts, because a slump often has you searching.

"And you're looking at anything," he says, "and you've got to stop that. You've got to shrink your world: small targets, and only let your closest confidants in. You could listen to what everybody says, but it better hit your back like water hitting a duck's back."

There was no light-bulb moment when all of a sudden everything made sense, but in 1994, there were four top-tens, including two second-place finishes, and the following year, he won for the first time in close to a decade. But the real fireworks would come between 1998 and 2001, when he won six times past the age of forty—the most memorable of those coming in March 2000.

The clip has been played countless times on television. Sutton standing in the middle of the eighteenth fairway in the TPC Sawgrass and growling at the ball he had just hit with a six-iron: "Be the right club. Be the right club today!"

It was. Sutton did the unthinkable. He beat Tiger Woods, who was in the midst of a remarkable season when he won nine tournaments, including three majors. "I think at that time," Sutton says, "everybody was buying into the fact that nobody could ever beat him. And Tiger needed to be beat at that time—by anybody, and it was kind of a victory for everybody in a way."

Perhaps so, but even though there was another win the next month in Greensboro and one more the following year in Houston, his second career Players championship had enormous personal meaning. "I had been as far down in my career as you could put a person in the mid-1990s," he says, "and then to come back to that point was pretty gratifying for me. I mean, 1998 to 2000 was the best player that Hal Sutton ever was—that's the best way I can put it."

Sutton and I are sitting in a hospitality tent at the Ryder Cup matches in Louisville.

"How did it all happen?" I ask him.

"I think the older you get," he says, "and you have lived more life, you have a tendency to look both ways, and I think that's one of the things that causes slumps. You look back too much. You're comparing yourself to what you've already done. As you mature and you're more successful, you know what the consequences are of not performing. That's a scary thing."

And when you're struggling, it's natural, Sutton thinks, to grasp for help. But he made the mistake of thinking that anybody who offered had the answer, rather than relying more on himself.

"Anybody who gets to the eighteenth tee here," he motions out the window and down the fairway, "they're going to look around for help, and there ain't going to be anybody there."

The Ryder Cup it is a strange paradox in Sutton's life. For all the talk of his late-career triumph and the big titles he's won, he looks at the 1999 Ryder Cup as perhaps the high point. "I didn't think I'd ever make another Ryder Cup team [after 1987]," he says. "I didn't think it was going to ever be in me to do that again." He went 3-1-1 and earned more points than any other American in what may well be the most remarkable Ryder Cup effort ever.

But then came the disaster of 2004. Sutton captained an American team at Oakland Hills, which was trounced 18½ to 9½. It was the most lopsided loss ever by a United Sates Ryder Cup side, and the lowlight was the much-ballyhooed but ineffective pairing of Tiger Woods and Phil Mickelson, for which Sutton was vilified. "Captain Clueless," screamed the headlines.

"We put entirely too much importance on the captain," he says. "If the guys don't show up to play, you can't win.

What can a captain do? You can't pair people wrong if they're playing well. You can't pair them right if they're not. It's impossible."

Sutton had earlier told me that the arrival together of his career rebirth and parenthood, both late in life, was hardly a coincidence. A father of four, he'd had his first child at age thirty-eight.

"Kids make you feel at your lowest moment like you're still great," he says, "because you're their dad. And there's something very healthy about that, because in a sport like this there are times when you feel like you're the worst.

"You've got my career right there," he says referring to the sheet of paper I'm holding, which details his career results on the PGA Tour. "There were a few of those years right there where I felt like my life couldn't have been any worse. But if I'd had kids, it would have been a different story."

A dozen years later, his most recent marriage has broken down. He declines to talk about it other than to say that after four tries he's done with the institution. "There's a generation between Ashley and me," he says of the woman he married in 1994, "and it didn't seem monumental until I got to be fifty and she got to be thirty-five. As I got into my later forties it became apparent, there were some things I didn't want to relive, and there were some things she didn't want to miss. My kids love me, so I can go forward with that."

Wounded but wiser, the man once thought to be the

next Nicklaus sets out to re-create himself again on the Champions Tour after turning fifty in 2008.

"All I could tell anybody that was trying to be successful in anything is: don't take your eye off *your* ball," he says. "Your ball. That's the most important part, because we can start juggling a lot of balls, and we don't know which one we're fixing to hit. There's only one that you're playing. Keep your eye on your ball."

EPILOGUE

So if you've gotten this far, you're probably wondering: did it work? Well, I don't think Tiger Woods is looking over his shoulder, but I'm a lot better off than I was. I've come in off the ledge. I've learned an awful lot—about the game, myself, and life in general.

When I first started in television, a friend told me that however slowly and deliberately I was speaking, it wasn't anywhere near as slowly and deliberately as I *thought* I was speaking. In other words, take your foot off the accelerator. It proved to be the most valuable piece of technical advice I've ever heard. In the past year, I've come to realize that the same advice is not only the essential first step in climbing out of a slump, but pretty good strategy for almost everything in life. Think about it. Wouldn't most of what we do end up better if we just didn't hurry through it so much?

"I think the most important thing is that people get anxious," Arnold Palmer told me. "Just slow down." Arnold suggests that if you slow down *everything* you do—walking, talking, even tying your shoes—your overall behavior can perhaps help slow down the central and operative culprit in a slump: the tempo of your golf swing.

"Why so hard?" Roger Maltbie pleaded to know from me one day when my hypersonic swing produced yet another undistinguished result. "No one ever hit the ball with their backswing. It's just foreplay. Slow down your backswing!"

My friend and colleague Gary Koch, who has about as nice a swing as you can build, often talks about something Al Geiberger once passed along to him. Physics dictates that there's only one point in the golf swing at which it can be moving its fastest, and you want that to be at impact, certainly not in your backswing or just as you start your downswing.

Ernie Els, "The Big Easy," swings so effortlessly that you'd swear that what just produced that 175-yard seven-iron was only a practice swing. Yet, he's one of the longer hitters in all of golf. I'm kind of thinking that's not exactly a coincidence.

I can't help thinking back on the lesson Davis Love Jr. learned from his college coach, Harvey Penick: If there's a practice green at your driving range, try and hit more club than you need to land the ball on that green. If the target area is 155 yards away, and that's a distance for which you'd normally use a seven-iron, use a five-iron instead. You'll be forced to swing more easily and thus reinforce the feeling of an easy, unforced tempo.

And maybe the best golf tip I've ever heard has to do with tempo. Jim Flick, the venerable instructor who's worked with—among others—Jack Nicklaus, says you should be able to feel the weight of the club head throughout your entire swing. Try it. There's no way you can do it if you swing too fast.

I've done a lot of looking around in the past year, and I've come to the conclusion that while there are a lot of things that turn our golf games upside down, tempo is the place where the discussion needs to start. In other words, no matter how slowly and deliberately you are swinging, you're not swinging anywhere near as slowly and deliberately as you *think* you're swinging.

A slump is a frightening thing, but as player after player told me: don't panic.

That might seem like reasonable advice while you're sitting in an easy chair reading a book, but considerably harder while standing in the middle of the eighth fairway, just having shanked a seven-iron. Tom Watson, citing Penick's wisdom, says: If you have one bad round of golf, just forget about it. If you have two straight bad rounds, you might want to start thinking about it. A third consecutive bad round of golf, and it's time to get some help.

But just because you're going to seek help doesn't mean that you have to demolish your swing and start from scratch. I'm always wary when I go to an instructor who wants me to subscribe to *their* swing theory rather than diagnosing what's specifically wrong with *my* swing and trying to fix it.

There are a million ways to swing the club. Jack Nicklaus told me that the best ball striker he'd ever seen was Lee Trevino. You'd never teach somebody to swing like Trevino, or Palmer, or Ray Floyd for that matter, but that doesn't mean they don't have effective swings. Between them, they've won seventeen major championships.

"I look at a lot of the golf swings on Tour," says Justin Rose, "and I actually don't know how they function. There are some clubs in some very bad positions. But I guess they're repeatable, and guys believe in themselves and create that type of mental freedom that gives them the ability for that swing to be repeatable and reliable."

At the heart of the panic that often accompanies a slump is perhaps the most terrifying thought any golfer might ever conjure: What if I never get it back?

Despite our worst fears, that—according to almost everyone I spoke with—is unlikely. You don't just forget how to play. But resurrecting your game might take some work, and, in a vicious and ironic circle, that's exactly where another problem often arises.

Somehow, we've come to believe that throwing hours and energy at an issue should make it go away. But in golf, as with so many other things, it's not as much about the quantity of work as it is the quality. And too often this kind of feverish approach gives birth to a kind of hopeless anxiety. The harder you try, the harder it gets.

Davis Love Jr.'s words come to mind: Try less hard. I think he's right. One night not long after I'd started to write this book, I ran into a friend I hadn't seen in ages at the club I belong to. Dr. Anthony Pisacano is an enormously successful eye surgeon, but he's also the type of guy whose picture and phone number should be posted in the marketing and sales departments of any organization selling golf cure-all gizmos or advice manuals. I swear he's tried everything. The permanent image of Tony I have seared in my brain is a pained grimace immediately upon completion of his swing, usually accompanied by an expletive or a loud cry of frustration.

"How's your golf?" I ask him.

"Actually, not bad," he answers in an almost Zen-calm manner.

"What?! Jeez, Tony," I say. "I don't know that I've ever heard you this positive about your game. What's this all about? Did you find the secret?"

"I think I just stopped giving a shit so much," he replies.

So here is this highly successful and motivated man, who's spent thousands on lessons and equipment and logged just as many hours on the range practicing, all in the quixotic pursuit of golf happiness, and he finds that the answer is to "just let it go" a little bit more.

Some of the greatest players of all time found that letting go of the game needs to be literal. When he was struggling, Arnold Palmer took weeks off. Jack Nicklaus took off months.

"The first thing you've got to do when you're having a problem is get away from it," Nicklaus told me.

In the summer of 2008, I had a chance to test drive that solution, although it wasn't by choice. Between the middle of July and the beginning of September, I didn't so much as touch a club. Between Wimbledon, the Summer Olympics in Beijing, and a few other assignments, I was constantly traveling. My first week back, I went to Westchester Country Club to see Harvey Lanack, who made a few observations. The next day, I played eighteen holes at Sunningdale Country Club with my friend and colleague Michael Weisman of NBC Sports. It was a mostly successful day until I violated the advice Dan Jansen had given me. Laying three in a greenside bunker of the par-five eighteenth hole, I bladed a sand wedge over the green and closed with a triple bogey for 88.

"Be in the moment," Dan had said. "Most of my bad shots I can trace back to being distracted in some way, not giving the matter at hand *total* attention."

Digging in over my ball in that bunker, I suppose that thinking about beating the traffic, and wondering what I might make my family for dinner that evening, probably weren't the best swing thoughts.

I don't think there was a single person I talked to who didn't recognize the importance of the game's mental aspect. Ben Crenshaw offered the old Bobby Jones quote: "The hardest course of all is only five inches long—the one between your ears."

There was a shag-bag full of good thoughts on this issue.

"Invest in your mind," said Justin Rose. "It's a muscle; it needs to be exercised."

From Steve Stricker: "Your swing is a product of your mind. Keep a positive attitude."

From David Duval: "At all costs, protect your confidence."

This last point can't be emphasized enough, and baseball Hall of Famer Mike Schmidt is the perfect example. The former Phillies third baseman has been playing golf since he was a kid, but he only took it up seriously upon retiring from baseball in 1989. Blessed with extraordinary hand–eye coordination that enabled him to hit 548 home runs, Schmidt poured himself into the game and now carries a USGA handicap index of plus 2.3. At the Leatherstocking Golf Course near the Hall of Fame in Cooperstown, New York, 6,500 yards from the back tees, he's shot 64, and, he says, "67 a few times on *legitimate* courses." But despite twenty years of "grinding" to play real tournament golf, he's never won a tournament.

"I'm a seriously ridiculous underachiever as a golfer," he says. And when things go wrong, there's really no mystery.

"There's something missing about my belief in myself as a player that will surface," he says. "Negativity will surface and will somehow bring me down." As a baseball player, Schmidt knew he could correct any flaws that put him in a slump, but as a golfer, despite his extraordinary talent, he's not sure.

"My position would be: here we go again," he says. " I had this shit cured. I thought I was over this. Every golfer has to battle through that sense that he's inadequate."

So maybe golf's mental battle is the most important part of the puzzle, but it's not that simple. "If it was only about what goes on in your head," says Paul Azinger, "then [Dr] Bob Rotella would be the world's best player."

As golfers we're so desperate that we think the answer is hopelessly hidden, whereas in fact, when it comes to mechanics, it's right under our noses. Actually, it's at our fingertips, literally. "I see so many bad grips," says Ben Crenshaw, "and it's so important. It's the one thing all instructors seem to agree on."

And it isn't only the grip. The first thing so many good players said they did when they started to struggle was to go back and examine the *first* things they learned in golf: the fundamentals, grip alignment, and ball position. The great philosopher Maltbie notes that fundamentals are all the things we do *before* we put the club in motion.

Hank Haney, Tiger Woods' coach, is amazed that people don't pay enough attention to alignment, especially because as TV-watching golfers we are a monkey-see, monkey-do bunch.

"You watch professionals, and every single one of them—without exception—walks into his setup from behind the ball," says Haney. "Doesn't matter if it's a putt, doesn't matter what kind of shot it is. They always start every shot off from *behind* the ball—and yet most amateurs walk up to the ball from the *side*. So you have one way that every touring pro in the history of the game has done things, and yet 95 percent of the amateurs don't do it that way, and it's the simplest thing, before you even go into motion or hit the golf ball. That's kind of amazing."

About slumps, every golfer I knew had a thought on the best path to travel.

"Doesn't matter what level you're at or what sport you're in," Wayne Gretzky told me. "Every athlete goes through some type of down period of the season. And I think what separates the good players from the superstars is that the best players figure out a way to mentally and physically fight their way through it and get out of it quicker than the average athlete."

The "Great One" is now mostly a casual golfer, who enjoys the game with his wife and kids, all of whom play, but there was a time he was much more serious. After retiring in 1999, he spent two years working diligently at golf and got down to "about a seven" handicap. "One of my biggest prizes as an athlete," says the man who won four Stanley Cups and nine Hart Memorial Trophies for league MVP, "is [the trophy] I won for the net division of the Sherwood Country Club member golf championship. I was pretty proud to get my name on a plaque. They laugh at me down at the shop, but I'm pretty proud of that. They can't take it away."

While Gretzky thinks that to be the best requires dedication, regardless of the sport, he knows what helped him through the roughest times in hockey.

"You try and simplify the game as much as you can,' he says. "Instead of trying to meet people at the blue line, you try to get the puck in deep, and try to make sure you get it back. You don't make that extra move. So I found that just simplifying the game was a quicker way to get out of that feeling."

My friend George Duarte said the answer was simply to play golf with him. Somehow, he said, everyone who teed it up with him magically came out of their slump almost immediately.

And there so many great things I heard along the way.

From Johnny Miller: "Pressure is a privilege."

From Steve Stricker: "Nobody swings it perfect. Perfect is whatever you can repeat."

David Duval told me to work on my short game. Actually, he didn't so much tell me to work on my short game as much as he made a bold statement, which at first sounded ridiculous: "As a ten handicap, there's no reason you can't be as good chipping the ball as me." Off a good lie, with a little bit of green to work with, it shouldn't be that hard, he contends. "All you have to do is move the club about this far," he says putting his hands about two feet apart. "I mean, seriously." Duval also reminded me that you have to *think* about what you're doing, think about where the tee markers are pointing. "We throw so many shots away," he says.

And while we're on the topic of tee markers, why is it that so many men feel a macho compulsion to play from the back tees when they have no business being there? The last thing we need in our games is something to make it harder than it's supposed to be, especially if we're struggling. "All the way back is for very low handicap players," says Davis Love III. "Most people play too far back. I don't know why."

Love had wonderful uncomplicated wisdom to share and also great stories. My favorite, I thought, had nothing to do with slumps, but maybe it had everything to do with learning how to get the best out of yourself.

When he was an undergraduate at the University of North Carolina, Love became friendly with Buzz Peterson, a guard on the basketball team, who loved to play golf. Peterson's roommate got to be curious about the game, and Michael Jordan hasn't been able to shake his curiosity yet. And Jordan wasn't the only one. You'd figure that a team good enough to win the NCAA championship in 1982 would spend all the time it possibly could in the gym practicing. But several of the Tar Heel players got hooked on golf. It got to be so extreme that one day Love was walking across campus when he bumped into Dean Smith, the legendary UNC basketball coach, who himself is an inveterate golfer. It was time for practice, and although he couldn't find his players, he thought he knew exactly where they were.

"Davis, I need you to do something for me," the coach told Love. "Will you send all the basketball team back up to the gym? They're all on the golf course." Love told him the players were "kind of having fun." They were just taking a break from the thing they were grinding to perfect. Maybe, like Nicklaus and Palmer, they were just stepping away for a bit.

All this said, there really is no universal prescription for a slump. Aspirin mostly works for a headache, but instruction/advice is more like choosing the proper antibiotic for an infection. Something will just seem to make more sense than everything else. It's like walking through a marketplace where everyone is babbling in a foreign language, and then suddenly, amidst the incomprehensible din, you'll hear a voice clearly speaking in your native tongue.

For me, one of those moments came when I was listening to Karen Palacios-Jansen, Dan Jansen's wife. She was talking about how, when she met Dan, before he started to make real progress with his game, he didn't really understand the importance of the grip. How its position at the top of the swing entirely determines how the hands arrive at impact.

Bingo!

And enough can't be said about keeping a positive outlook, even in the worst of times. Golf has given Greg Norman heartbreak enough to last a lifetime, yet he learned to look at things differently. "Show me a path without obstacles and that path leads nowhere," says the plaque on his desk. Paul Azinger came back from cancer to win on the PGA Tour! It may sound trite, but if you're really willing to dedicate yourself, you can probably do things you didn't think you could. George Herbert Walker Bush was shot down in the Pacific during World War II. As he floated in the water, wounded and surrounded by sharks and the enemy, a positive outlook might have been his lifeline.

If there's one thing I've learned in this journey of the past year, it is that slumps come and go. Ben Crenshaw said he was "gone twenty times," and *Golf Digest* said he's had more comebacks than John Travolta. It's not like you can get some kind of inoculation that provides lifetime immunity.

Golf, like life, is just too sweet to spend time mired in what's wrong, especially when you can do something to make it right.

If you choose to play this game, Marley's ghost will likely visit you from time to time. The trick is not letting those rattling chains scare you so much.

ACKNOWLEDGMENTS

In early December 2007, I called my sister Nancy and told her that I was going to write a book. For a moment, there was silence on the other end of the line and then she said, "I think mom and dad would have been happy if you'd just *read* a book." The sarcastic, loving, and accurate observation of an older sibling aside, the fact remains that writing a book is not only hard work, but also impossible to even contemplate without an enormous amount of help. And so thank you. . .

To Gil Caps, who helped make sure I got it right, down to the smallest detail. No one is a more knowledgeable or conscientious golf source.

To the best team in the game, my colleagues at NBC Sports: Tommy Roy, Tom Randolph, Doug Grabert, Joe Martin, Mary Muzina, Dan Hicks, Johnny Miller, Gary Koch, Bob Murphy, Dottie Pepper, Mark Rolfing, Roger Maltbie, Cathy Crowther, Sandra Baker, and

Jackie Moretti. The only thing that mitigates the sadness of leaving my family so often is that I know I'm heading towards my second family.

To my friends and respected colleagues from the golf writing and reporting community, who offered invaluable help, advice, and support for a novice author: Tim Rosaforte, John Feinstein, Dan Jenkins, Doug Ferguson, Jeff Babineau, John Hawkins, Bob Verdi, Bill Fields, and Geoff Russell.

To the good people of the PGA Tour staff—Dave Lancer, Joel Schuchmann, Dave Senko, Phil Stambaugh, Joe Chemycz, Chris Reimer, Nelson Silverio, John Bush, Laura Neal, Doug Milne, Joan T. Alexander, Anna Leaird, and Denise Taylor—who were so enormously helpful answering questions and locating difficult-to-find information. And to Julius Mason of the PGA of America.

To Mark Russell and Slugger White, of the PGA Tour's field staff, not only for their help interpreting certain aspects of the rules of golf, but also for their seemingly bottomless reservoir of good will.

To Bill Hughes and Paul Luthringer—real professionals who encouraged me and offered their invaluable help and friendship.

To my golf buddies—Stone Phillips and Greg Odland—who, I'm sorry to say, have seen it all.

To Peter Malik, for a lot of things.

To Holly McClure, and Mike Head, for staying up late

and always working so hard to make my broadcast essays the best they could possibly be.

To Bruce Nichols of HarperCollins, who enthusiastically embraced my idea. To Bill Strachan, who gently helped me shape it into something I'd be proud of.

To Scott Waxman, without whose support and energy this book wouldn't have existed. And to the always cheerful Melissa Sarver.

To Dr. Chris Lutz for keeping me on my feet.

To the special people in my life whom I'm fortunate to have: my sisters Jane Lindemann and Nancy Roberts, and to Rob Tiburzi, the brother I never had.

To all the people who made time for me and whose voices speak in these pages. It's easy to talk about the good times, but the uneasy details of the uncertain and less distinguished days and nights give this work its true character.

And to Scott Tolley, Doc Giffin, Scott Sayers, Marcus Day, Jim Appleby, and especially the incomparable Kevin Sullivan, thank you for helping make so many of these conversations possible.

But most of all, to Sandy, Jackson, Aidan, and Daniel, for letting me selfishly go away and chase the circus. It's so strange that after writing sixty thousand words, I can't seem to come up with just a handful more to adequately say how much I love you.